LEAD
LIKE BUTLER

John + Marti
May God bless you -

Kent Millard

LIKE BUTLER

Six Principles for Values–Based Leaders

KENT MILLARD & JUDITH CEBULA
FOREWORD BY COACH BRAD STEVENS

Abingdon Press

Nashville

LEAD LIKE BUTLER
SIX PRINCIPLES FOR VALUES-BASED LEADERS

Copyright © 2013 Abingdon Press

All rights reserved.

ISBN 978-1-4267-4914-8

13 14 15 16 17 18 19 20 21 22—10 9 8 7 6 5 4 3 2 1
MANUFACTURED IN THE UNITED STATES OF AMERICA

CONTENTS

· ·

FOREWORD

I was twenty-three years old when I decided to leave my job as a marketing associate at Eli Lilly to pursue a career in coaching. I had a few small-school opportunities, but ultimately chose to be a graduate manager at Butler University. I chose Butler (it's actually hard to say I chose something, when I was actually going to be paying to be there!) for two reasons. First, I believed in their newly appointed head coach, Thad Matta, whom I had met working Butler's basketball camps. Second, I was intrigued by the Butler program and its success in the late 1990s. Even though I was raised right up the road, had worked camps, and considered myself a fan of the program, I couldn't pinpoint what had transformed Butler from a solid program to one that could play with the biggest programs on any stage. My curiosity was quenched almost immediately after I joined the program.

In the spring of 2000, I walked into the locker room, and the first thing I noticed was a sign on the wall listing five core values. It was relayed to me that those core values had adorned that wall since 1997. In the mid-90s, Butler Head Coach Barry Collier (current athletic director) traveled with Bowling Green's Jim Larranaga to meet with Wisconsin head coach, Dick Bennett. Coach Bennett had a very accomplished coaching career at UW-Stevens Point and UW-Green Bay before becoming the head coach at Wisconsin. He was renowned for his game coaching and his offensive and defensive strategies. However, what struck Coach Collier most about that summer meeting was Bennett's emphasis on the importance of his five core values: Passion, Unity, Servanthood, Thankfulness, and Humility. All biblical in nature, these values were at the foundation of Coach Bennett's program. And in the past decade and a half, these values have guided Butler basketball to new heights.

Coach Collier was the architect of this culture. As a head coach, he ran a values-based program that became one of the most respected in the country. And now as an administrator, he embodies and embraces those very same values that lead him to such great success as a coach. By doing so, he has created an environment in which his employees feel empowered to work hard and do things the right way. Spend time with him, and you immediately know that he loves Butler and wants it to thrive in the long term.

Initiated by Coach Tony Hinkle, led by Barry Collier, coined by Thad Matta, and first defined by Todd Lickliter, The Butler Way was introduced as a slogan to describe our desire to strive in a values-based basketball program. In the year 2000, I was sitting in Coach Lickliter's office with the door closed, scribbling down notes on how to define our program's mission, vision, and The Butler Way.

That attempt to define The Butler Way included the following bullet points to hammer home what is required to play basketball at Butler:

- Place the well-being of teammates before individual desires
- Embrace the process of growth
- Execute the Butler system
- Demonstrate toughness in every circumstance

It's fun for me to think back to those meetings in Coach Lickliter's office and to all of the thought that he put into building on the culture at Butler. As was the case with his predecessors, his desire to do great work continues to impact Butler every day, and played a large role in success on and off the court.

As I reflect on my years at Butler, I'm thankful for all the great people I had a chance to work with and coach. Our coaching staffs and administrative staffs were terrific. Our players were awesome to coach. I feel indebted to those head coaches who came before me because those values and thoughts that adorn the walls are things that have helped me grow as a person, a husband, a father, and a coach. As we always told our players, when you play at Butler, there's a responsibility to represent your school and this program to the very best of your ability. You have the road map. If you do that, you'll have a great experience, and your highlights will continue long past your time as a college basketball player.

—Brad Stevens

INTRODUCTION

It was a David-versus-Goliath basketball story.

The Duke University Blue Devils of Durham, North Carolina, was the top-seeded team, superbly coached by the legendary Mike Krzyzewski. "Coach K" was seeking his fourth national championship title with some of the biggest, most talented, and toughest players in all of college basketball. They were expected to win—and win big.

The Butler University men's basketball team, meanwhile, was fifth-seeded. They had entered the 2010 National Collegiate Athletic Association Division I tournament with a 200:1 chance of winning the championship. They were coached by a thirty-three-year-old named Brad Stevens who was in his third year at Butler. Coach Stevens looked so young he was often mistakenly identified as one of his players. At six foot nine, Butler's tallest player had to go up against a seven-foot-one Duke giant.

Butler University had already shocked the basketball world by defeating another one-seed team, Syracuse, and a strong two-seed team, Kansas State, on their way to the championship game. Butler had become the smallest school (enrollment: 4,200) to play in the championship game in the forty-year history of the NCAA tournament. Along the way, they had become the archetypical Cinderella team, as people from all over the world cheered for this unheralded team from Indianapolis that miraculously won game after game that they were predicted to lose.

On April 5, 2010, 71,000 people packed Lucas Oil Stadium in Indianapolis, about five miles from the Butler University campus. Forty-eight million U.S. television viewers, and millions more in 178 countries around the world, tuned in for this David-versus-Goliath game.

It was close and hard fought. With two minutes left, Duke held a 60-55 lead. Butler took advantage of a Duke traveling call and scored. Duke missed their next shot, Butler scored again, then Duke made one free throw. The score was Duke 61, Butler 59, with a mere 3.6 seconds on the clock.

The young but calm Butler coach, Brad Stevens, called a time-out and gathered his team on the side of the court. He said, "Stay poised. We're going to win this game."

Six-foot-nine guard Gordon Hayward received the inbound pass and dribbled to the center of the court. Forty-five feet from the basket, he let go of a jump shot. The clock expired. Millions of people around the world stood on their feet and held their breath. Later, it was determined that if Hayward's shot had been an inch to the left, Butler would have won one of the most dramatic games in basketball history. Instead, it clanged off the rim of the basket and bounced out. Duke won, 61-59.

After the game, a Duke player said, "Those guys can flat-out play basketball!" Duke University walked off the court with the championship trophy in their hands. The Butler team walked off the court as champions in the hearts of millions of people around the world.

Sportswriters from all over the world descended on Indianapolis, both the site of the championship game and the location of Butler University, to find out more about this small college that almost upset one of the perennially premier basketball programs in the nation. Many of them celebrated Butler University's one time in the spotlight, noting that they would likely never make it to an NCAA championship game again.

A year later, Butler University proved them wrong. Not only did they receive a return invitation to the NCAA tournament, they again defeated much higher-ranked opponents to reappear in the championship game. Even casual sports fans were amazed to see the Butler Bulldogs playing in the championship game two years in a row. The sequel did not go according to Butler's script, though. Butler University lost the 2011 championship game by twelve points to the University of Connecticut, again becoming the runner-up.

Curiosity about the story of Butler survived the final score. Observers from around the world wondered how this small, little-known university in the Midwest had achieved what few schools have ever done: making it to the final championship game two years in a row. People wanted to know more about Butler University and its amazing basketball team.

The team defied the conventional wisdom of successful, high-profile college basketball teams. They did not have the most famous college players in the nation. They attended class and sported one of the highest grade-point averages of any NCAA basketball team. Sportswriters reported that when the championship game was played in Indianapolis in 2010, all of the Butler team members attended their college classes during the day before taking the court on national television that night.

When a group of individuals in any arena of life does well, one of the keys to understanding their success is to examine the leadership practices of the key leaders of that team. Much of the curiosity has been focused on first-time head coach and team leader, Brad Stevens. Stevens coaches according to a set of principles, or values, broadly known as The Butler Way.

The Butler Way did not spring up overnight. Coach Stevens points out that he did not invent or create the values and principles that are articulated in this book. He says that he is simply leading by principles that many former leaders have pondered, articulated, and practiced.

The source of the principles, according to Stevens, is Coach Tony Hinkle, whose name sits above the university arena. Over the course of thirty-six years, from 1934 to 1970, the iconic Coach Hinkle served as the athletic director and the football, basketball, and baseball coach at Butler. In his book, *Tony Hinkle: A Coach For All Seasons*, newscaster Howard Caldwell stated that no coach in America has been involved with more athletes in more sports over a longer period of time.

Coach Hinkle developed a much-copied strategic approach to the game of basketball, characterized by highly disciplined defense and rapid offensive ball movement, where everyone moves, everyone handles the ball, and everyone has a chance to shoot. Many say this is still a chief characteristic of Butler basketball. However, Coach Hinkle is mostly remembered as a highly principled coach who encouraged players to set high standards for themselves both on and off the court. Coaches from all over the nation came to learn the Hinkle system, which produced winning teams, sometimes with modest talent. Butler University consistently produced athletes who sought to uphold high standards in their personal lives. Coach Stevens considers Coach Hinkle one of the most remarkable college coaches because he taught players to put the well-being of the team above themselves, to put selfishness aside, and to work for constant personal improvement for the sake of the team.

The first Butler team to make the NCAA tournament was Tony Hinkle's 1961–1962 Bulldogs. Like the recent Butler teams, they were undersized underdogs who nevertheless won games they weren't expected to win. A February 2, 1962, *Time* magazine article labeled the team "Fierce Little Butler." The article pointed out that the starting five averaged only six-one and included five-eight and five-nine guards. Coach Hinkle acknowledged that their opponents were always taller, but he told his team, "They put their pants on the same way we put them on. They just pull them up higher."

On February 12, 2012, twelve members of the 1962 Butler team returned to Hinkle Fieldhouse for a fifty-year reunion. The unranked Bulldogs defeated highly ranked rivals like Bowling Green and Western Kentucky before falling to number three-ranked Kentucky in the 1962 NCAA tournament. When asked how they won against higher-ranked teams, Ken Freeman, now seventy-two years old, said, "There was better cohesiveness on that team than you could ever imagine. Everyone was for everyone else and the team. We would have tried to run through a wall for each other."[1]

Jeff Blue, another player on that 1962 team, said about Coach Hinkle, "He was a great teacher. Even in the heat of battle, he would start drawing a play in chalk on the floor—even to do things we hadn't practiced....He really had the faith. It turns out we could execute what he wanted on the spur of the moment."[2]

Butler Athletic Director Barry Collier and Coach Brad Stevens constantly remind interviewers that they are simply trying to implement the values-based coaching style initiated by the legendary Butler coach Tony Hinkle.

Basketball coach John Wooden, who won twelve national championships at Indiana State University and UCLA, also influenced Coach Stevens. Like Hinkle,

Coach Wooden was a values-based coach and leader who wanted his players not just to do well on the court, but to succeed in the game of life. Wooden made statements like:

> Be more concerned with your character than your reputation, because your character is what you really are, while your reputation is merely what others think you are. Material possessions, winning scores, and great reputations are meaningless in the eyes of the Lord, because he knows what we really are, and that is all that matters.[3]

Coach Tony Dungy, former coach of the Indianapolis Colts professional football team, served as a mentor and model for Coach Stevens in leading young men to develop high character values as a part of their athletic experience. In his book *Quiet Strength*, Dungy writes:

> It's about the journey—mine and yours—and the lives we can touch, the legacy we can leave, and the world we can change for the better.[4]

In *The Mentor Leader*, Coach Dungy writes:

> Remember that Mentor Leadership is all about serving. Jesus said, "For even the Son of Man came not to be served but to serve and to give his life as a ransom for many" (Mark 10:45).[5]

Coach Barry Collier, current athletic director and former player and coach at Butler University, spoke of values-based coaching and leadership during his Butler coaching days as well. Indeed, it was Collier, while men's basketball coach in the 1990s, who shaped what he learned playing for George Theofanis into what is known today as The Butler Way. It grew from a series of weekend retreats he made to Wisconsin to visit another legendary college coach, Dick Bennett, then leading the University of Wisconsin-Madison. Inspired at first by Bennett's success on the court, Collier wanted to learn about the teaching principles that drove those Wisconsin teams to victory. Bennett told of five simple, enduring ideas: humility, passion, teamwork, service, and gratitude. He shared with Collier a laminated single-page playbook that contained these values. But behind these values was a rich collection of Scripture verses. Coaching at public schools his entire career, Bennett rarely used Christian language to explain his approach, but faithfulness to the lessons of Jesus was always at the core.

Collier was inspired to bring the focus on these virtues back to Butler, where, after all, he had learned them playing for Tony Hinkle. But it would take Collier's successor, Thad Matta, to write the five values of humility, passion, unity, servanthood, and thankfulness down and post them on an athletic department wall as a way to remind himself, his coaching staff, and his team of the values on which they based their team and their lives. Successor Coach Todd Lickliter continued to refine the meaning of these values during his time as head coach. When Coach Stevens rose from assistant coach to head coach in 2007 at age thirty, he carried on the tradition of modeling these values personally and putting them into practice—and adding one more: accountability.

Coach Stevens uses a pyramid, modeled after John Wooden's pyramid, to illustrate how those six values lead to the success of his team.

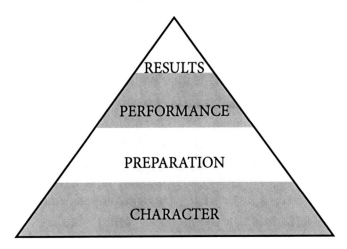

Positive character traits form the base of the pyramid. When a player practices the principles of Humility, Passion, Unity, Servanthood, Thankfulness, and Accountability, it creates positive character traits that turn into effective teamwork on the court and effective life after basketball. Stevens says that he wants players on his team who have positive character traits as well as good athletic ability. He wants to build teammates who play well on the court and are good students and good citizens off the court. Positive character traits are developed when coaches and players consistently live out the six principles of a values-based life.

The second layer on the pyramid is preparation. Coach Stevens and his players prepare intensely for playing basketball at a very high level. Stevens says he is up every morning by five o'clock, studying tapes of his team and the opponents they will play and designing strategies that will help them be successful on the court. In practice, players repeatedly go over strategies for effective defense, developing plays to create open shots, and working on inbound plays from various parts of the court. It is clear that Stevens and his players prepare intensely and consistently so that playing a high-quality game of basketball becomes second nature. Coach Stevens goes by the adage that teams that fail to prepare, prepare to fail.

The third layer of the pyramid is performance; actually performing in the game as well as you can. Stevens has been called a basketball savant because of his great knowledge about basketball strategies, which he uses for on-the-spot coaching. He depends on his team to move the ball around quickly until a player on his team can take an open shot.

The peak of the pyramid—the smallest part of the pyramid—is results. Most people simply focus on results: Did you win or lose the game? However, while Coach Stevens and his team want to win every game, they realize that they cannot always obtain the results they want. Ten highly motivated players moving in different directions at the same time creates many on-court variables in any particular game. While coaches can't determine the results, they can work on developing positive character traits among their players, preparing them well and coaching them to perform at their very best.

Sometimes Coach Stevens has been proud of his team in a loss because they practiced the character values well, they prepared well, and they performed well. Other times he is upset with his team in a win because they did not practice the character values as well as they could have. Important to Stevens is the fact that in time, wins and losses fade away, but the character values gained through playing for Butler University basketball will stay with his players and help them live effective and productive lives.

As an example, Coach Stevens related a story about one of his experiences in recruiting a player. The recruit was a good basketball player Coach Stevens wanted to have on his team. The coach began the conversation by asking the player what he wanted to do with his life after college: what were his goals and dreams for his profession after he finished his basketball career?

The player explained his interest in pursuing a certain profession after he finished his basketball career. Coach Stevens responded that for the young athlete's specific major, other universities besides Butler might better prepare him for his future career. He explained that while he wanted him on his team, what he wanted even more was that this player might be well prepared for his life after basketball, even though it might mean attending and playing for a different team.

Stevens practices a countercultural approach to recruiting athletes. Many coaches may seek to convince players to attend their school because they want the players to help their team become successful. However, Coach Stevens wants situations for his players where being on the Butler team and getting a degree from Butler will help them be successful in their future lives. He is focused on how playing on the Butler team will help a student succeed in life, not on how he can use a student athlete to help his team be more successful.

It is clear that Coach Stevens personally practices the values of humility, passion, unity, service, thankfulness, and accountability. This book articulates the six leadership values taught across the board by the men's and women's basketball coaches and assistant coaches at Butler University. Each chapter of the book is devoted to exploring one of the values through interviews with coaches, players, and alumni. Our hope is to explore the specific ways they form the foundation of success for coaches and players both on the basketball court and in their life journey after basketball.

Coach Brad Stevens; his wife, Tracy; and their two children are active members of St. Luke's United Methodist Church in Indianapolis, where Dr. Kent Millard served as Senior Pastor from 1993 to 2011. Coach Stevens demonstrates his commitment to service by volunteering his time in serving in a church soup kitchen. He often donates his time to speak to various groups in the church and community about character values and his faith. Judith Cebula is the Director of the Center for Faith and Vocation at Butler University and a former newspaper religion reporter. Coach Stevens has been an encourager and speaker for students and faculty involved in promoting faith on the Butler campus and encouraging students and faculty to pursue the vocation to which they feel called by their faith tradition.

We are honored to explore the benefits of values-based leadership through this book and want to encourage people—of all faith traditions or even of no faith tradition—to practice humility, passion, unity, service, thankfulness, and accountability, with the goal of creating more values-based leaders in our world.

Dr. Kent Millard

Ms. Judith Cebula

Friday, April 27, 2012

HUMILITY

You can accomplish anything in life, provided that you do not mind who gets the credit.
—*President Harry S. Truman*

Level five leaders demonstrate humility and a compelling modesty, shun public adulation, and are never boastful.
—*Jim Collins,* Good to Great

Do nothing from selfish ambition or conceit, but in humility regard others as better than yourselves.
—*Paul of Tarsus (Phil. 2:3 NRSV)*

Happy are people who are humble, because they will inherit the earth.
—*Jesus (Matt. 5:5)*

Each summer the Butler University men's basketball team conducts a skills camp for elementary and junior high school students. At the camp, Coach Brad Stevens and his wife, Tracy, work in the cafeteria line on the first night, serving food to the young players and their parents who come through.

1

On one occasion, a mother of a prospective student came through the line to receive her food. She looked intently at Coach Stevens and said, "I think I have seen you someplace before. Are you connected with the Butler basketball team?"

Coach Stevens replied, "Yes, I am connected to the team."

The woman replied, "Good! Maybe you can tell me more about Blue [the Butler bulldog mascot]. Will we get to see him at the camp?"

Coach Stevens told her he also liked Blue but that Blue would not be at the camp. The woman said, "I just love that bulldog!"

She walked off, never knowing that the head basketball coach and his wife had served her food and answered her questions.

Brad later relayed this story to his team and reminded them not to think too highly of themselves. Some of their fans are more interested in the bulldog mascot than in the players on the team!

No Task Is Too Unimportant

Many head coaches simply show up at their basketball camps to say a few words of welcome. Coach Stevens and his wife put on an apron and serve. Their simple act speaks loudly to the Butler players and the young camp participants. When players see their head coach behind the counter serving food, they receive an important message: no task is too demeaning or unimportant when it makes a contribution to the well-being of others.

The players who make it on the Butler basketball team have all been high school basketball stars and have received various awards for their outstanding athletic abilities. They often come to college with a fairly high opinion of their ability and talent. When players have a high opinion of their existing abilities, it is often difficult to teach them a new system for playing basketball. If they are overfilled with pride in their own abilities, they may be resistant to learning a new role on a new team.

Humble people, however, are teachable people who realize that there is always more for them to learn. They are open and willing to learn new skills in the game of basketball. They are willing to acknowledge they can grow and increase in their basketball skills as well as in their life skills.

In every field of life, those who are filled with pride and arrogance are usually not open to new learning because they believe they know all there is to know about their area of work. Truly great people are those who are humble enough to be open to new growth and learning in their lives.

Genuine humility has been defined as realizing at the core of our being that we are not superior to anyone else and that we are not inferior to anyone else. Externally, we have differing abilities and talents, but as persons created in the image of God, we are all of equal value in the sight of God.

A History of Humility

When asked how these principles became such a significant part of the Butler athletic program, Coach Stevens refers to Butler's athletic director, Barry Collier.

At six foot seven, Barry Collier was a star athlete at Palmetto High School in Miami, Florida. After graduation he played basketball at Miami Dade, where he received a two-year Associate of Arts degree. Collier then transferred to Butler University, located in Indianapolis, Indiana, because he was deeply impressed with Hinkle Fieldhouse, Butler's huge basketball arena, and the importance of basketball in the Hoosier state. He played two years as center and forward at Butler on teams that were not particularly outstanding.

After graduation, Collier received his M.S. degree from Indiana University and then served as an assistant basketball coach at several different universities around the nation. In 1989, Collier returned to Butler University as the men's head basketball coach and served for eleven years.

The first two years as head coach were disappointing for Coach Collier. In his first year, the team won six games and lost twenty-two. The second year was not much better. Coach Collier and his team were very discouraged. So Collier went to see Coach Dick Bennett, who at the time was the head coach at the University of Wisconsin in Madison, Wisconsin. Coach Bennett had been exceedingly successful as a basketball coach, and Collier hoped that he would learn some basketball strategies and secrets to help him improve his team.

Coach Bennett spent two days with Collier and Jim Larranaga, then coach at George Mason University. They talked about the underlying principles and values that coaches had to demonstrate and young players had to learn if they were to be successful on the basketball court and in life. It was from Coach Bennett that Collier learned the values of humility, passion, unity, servanthood, and thankfulness. These were principles that had guided Bennett as a coach for decades—from his earliest days teaching in public high schools on through to leading the University of Wisconsin to four appearances in the NCAA tournament. He coached the team to the Final Four in 2000. These virtues became the foundation of The Butler Way, even as they had proven to be a winning formula years earlier at different schools.

Inspiration for these virtues to become guiding principles in coaching began early for Bennett, when he was coaching at a high school in Eau Claire, Wisconsin. A former player had returned to the school in the mid-1960s to finish his training in graduate school. He then volunteered for Bennett and Bennett observed that the young man had a profound sense of peace about him, so profound that Bennett was compelled to ask where it came from. Then, in a quiet way he just talked about his Christian faith and how it had sustained him in good times and in bad times. From that point on, Bennett's faith took on a new dimension, as did his coaching.

Bennett had grown up Catholic in Pittsburgh, one of four boys in an Italian-American family. Mom stayed home with the kids. Dad worked in steel mills and later in a factory that made fire engines. Faith and hard work had long been cornerstones of life, he recalled. However, with a newfound connection between the two, Bennett soared as a coach. All of the schools were public universities where outward expression of religious values was not appropriate. Yet Bennett found a way through values-based coaching to live his faith.

Like Bennett, Coach Collier was a devoted follower of Jesus Christ and he realized that all the five values were based in the Scriptures. He compiled a list of verses supporting each of these values, which to this day he carries on a laminated slip of paper in his pocket. Coach Collier returned to Butler University inspired to teach these values to his team. His goal shifted from just winning games to developing character among the Butler players. He carries this list:

- HUMILITY: "Do nothing out of selfish ambition or vain conceit, but in humility consider others better than yourselves." Philippians 2:3 NIV

- PASSION: "Do you not know that in a race all the runners run, but only one gets the prize? Run in such a way to get the prize." 1 Corinthians 9:24 NIV

- UNITY: "If a kingdom is divided against itself, that kingdom cannot stand." Mark 3:24 NIV

- SERVANTHOOD: "As iron sharpens iron, so one man sharpens another." Proverbs 27:17 NIV

- THANKFULNESS: "Be joyful always, pray continually, give thanks in all circumstances, for this is God's will for you in Christ Jesus." 1 Thessalonians 5:16-18 NIV 1984

As Collier taught the five principles to his team, the Butler program turned around. During the next nine years of coaching, Collier's team had a winning season every year. The Bulldogs made it to the NCAA postseason tournament for the first time in thirty-four years and ended up with invitations to six postseason tournaments during his nine-year coaching stretch. A high-quality basketball program was under way at Butler.

Collier credits the program's turnaround to the mentoring of Coach Dick Bennett, which helped him rediscover and put into practice principles and values that had earlier been articulated by legendary coach Tony Hinkle at Butler. Later, Coach Collier became head coach at the University of Nebraska for six years, then returned to Butler University as the athletic director, in 2006.

In 2007, as athletic director, Coach Collier made the risky decision to hire a thirty-year-old Butler assistant coach named Brad Stevens as head coach of the Butler men's basketball team. Sports reporters and alumni around the nation questioned the wisdom of Collier's decision.

Most had never heard of his hire. Some felt that Butler could have pursued a nationally known coach with much more coaching experience and significantly improved their chances of developing a first-rate team. But Collier hired Brad Stevens.

Brad Stevens was born on October 22, 1976, and grew up in Zionsville, Indiana, a suburb of Indianapolis. He was a star player on the Zionsville Community High School basketball team, where he still holds school records for most points scored, most assists, most steals, and most three-point field goals.

Stevens studied economics and business at DePauw University, a United Methodist-affiliated university in Greencastle, Indiana. At DePauw he played point guard, earned multiple all-conference and academic all-conference awards, and was an Academic All-American nominee. His DePauw basketball coach described Brad as one of the most selfless, team-oriented players he had ever coached.

After graduating from DePauw in 1999, Stevens was hired by Eli Lilly and Company, in Indianapolis. With a good-paying position, Stevens had a bright future at one of the largest pharmaceutical companies in the world.

However, Brad Stevens's passion was basketball. He had a deep desire to become a basketball coach, so Stevens resigned the position at Lilly to pursue his passion. He took a serving job at an Applebee's restaurant and arranged to share an apartment with some other young men.

"Looking back, it looks like a great idea," Stevens later remarked. "At the time, I thought it was something I really wanted to try." Stevens became a volunteer assistant for the Butler basketball team and Coach Thad Matta.

Matta was the first head coach to actually post leadership principles on the wall of the men's basketball locker room and remind the coaches and players to practice them regularly. He left Butler the next year, however. Assistant coach Todd Lickliter was promoted to head coach for the 2001–2002 season, and in turn promoted Brad to an assistant coach position. Coach Todd Lickliter led six Butler squads with success, including two appearances in the Sweet 16 round of the sixty-four-team NCAA tournament, before resigning to become coach of the University of Iowa Hawkeyes. A pattern had evolved that when Butler University developed a successful basketball coach, the coach moved on to a larger and more prestigious basketball program. Barry Collier went to Nebraska, Thad Matta to Xavier, and Todd Lickliter to Iowa. Coach Stevens would break that pattern.

In 2007, he became the second youngest head coach in Division I basketball and his success was immediate. Stevens had thirty wins in his first year as a head basketball coach, becoming the third youngest head coach in NCAA history to have a thirty-win season. By 2010, Stevens had broken the NCAA record for the most wins in a coach's first three years. After leading his team to the NCAA Championship game in 2010, many universities approached Brad Stevens about leaving Butler. Many people expected that Stevens would follow in the footsteps of other Butler coaches and move on to a larger university with bigger and newer facilities, a larger budget for recruiting top-notch basketball players, and a much larger salary.

However, Brad and his wife, Tracy, loved the Butler program and The Butler Way and wanted to stay in the community where their family and friends lived and where they had a church home at St. Luke's United Methodist Church. Brad said, "Why would I leave the place I love?" In spite of lucrative offers to coach other places, Stevens modeled humility above large salaries and prestigious positions. He signed a contract to coach at Butler University for the next ten years, until the 2021–22 season.

The First Value

Butler Athletic Director Barry Collier says that humility is the foundation value for student athletes at Butler. Humility encourages players to honestly recognize strengths and weaknesses and opens them to improving their gifts and strengthening their weaknesses. Humility also helps the players recognize that they need each other and that none of them can accomplish their goals alone. Constant reminders come from the professionally printed signs on display in the team locker room. Humility, as with all aspirational values, must be practiced always if it is to be lived. Perfection is strived for, but never achieved.

One of the signs in the locker room has the word "humility" in large letters followed by a statement that describes a humble person: "Does his job to the best of his ability, regardless of circumstances." Coach Stevens explains that this means that each player is to give his best effort to the team all the time regardless of whether he is on the court or on the bench, whether he is given public praise or ignored.

American society often lifts up and honors loud and boastful leaders in government, business, sports, and religion, as if these are the most effective leaders in our world. However, self-righteous and arrogant leaders are the ones who often bring down businesses, government, sports teams, and congregations. Proverbs 16:18 says, "Pride comes before distaster, and arrogance before a fall." The wisdom of the Scriptures and the ages has provided example after example of leaders who were overimpressed with themselves and felt they were above the rules of morality and honesty that apply to others. Their pride and haughty spirit eventually led to their fall from leadership and power.

So the old story goes, there was once a group of clergy who gathered for a workshop and, as a simulation exercise, the leader asked them all to choose an imaginary role in an orchestra. One person felt that she would like to be the first violinist because that is the key instrument in leading all the other instruments in the orchestra. Another person said that he would like to play the bass drum because it helps set the cadence for the rest of the orchestra. Several said they would like to be the director of the orchestra because they felt that was the most important and influential position in the orchestra. However, one pastor thought for a while and then said he would like to be the music stand, the one to hold the sheet music so that others could make beautiful music.

The conversation became subdued, because they all recognized that while they had chosen the position or instrument that gave them honor and recognition, one person chose the lowest and most humble position, the music stand. While most had chosen a position that offered honor and recognition, one saw himself as the humble servant of others. Most of us do not automatically think about taking the role of the humble servant of others; yet, ironically, people willingly follow and admire leaders who are not primarily focused on their position, power, and prestige.

Leading with Humility

Current key leadership studies in business seem to be working on the same points that Butler University basketball program has been working on since the mid-1990s. Leaders who lead with a strong sense of personal humility engender strong and dedicated followers who also lead with a strong sense of personal humility and deep commitment to the goals and visions of the organization.

After a long-term study of companies in the United States that had outstanding growth over a fifteen-year period during both good and poor economic times and in times of key leadership transitions, Jim Collins, a recognized leadership expert, published his findings in the bestselling book, *Good to Great*.

Collins developed a leadership pyramid of five levels of leadership. Bottom level leaders are highly capable individuals who make productive contributions through their talent, knowledge, and skills. Level two leaders apply their skills by working effectively with others in a group setting. Level three leaders are competent managers who can organize people and resources toward the effective pursuit of predetermined objectives. Level four leaders catalyze commitment to a clear and compelling vision. The highest level of leaders Collins calls level five leaders. These leaders build enduring greatness in an organization through a blend of personal humility and professional will. All of the companies thriving during both economic upturns and downturns had level five leaders who were characterized by personal humility and a deep commitment to their organization.

Collins noted that during interviews when level five leaders were complimented for the success of their companies, they always responded that success was dependent on the talent and commitment of their coworkers. He described these humble leaders as looking out the window of their offices toward their coworkers, crediting them in times of success. Those same leaders, when mistakes were made, looked at the same windows in their offices and saw a mirror reflecting only their own image. For faltering companies, the level five CEO *assumed responsibility*. Collins describes this trait as genuine personal humility that others recognize, admire, and follow.

That same humility that Butler encourages, that helps

the players recognize that none of them can accomplish their goals alone, is evident in successful leaders in business.

During his first year as Butler University president in 2012, James Danko recommended that Butler leaders read James O'Toole's book *Leading Change: The Argument for Values-Based Leadership*. It has been a formative text for Danko, who earned an undergraduate degree in religion at a Catholic Jesuit university, John Carroll University. Later he became an entrepreneur, leading a health and corporate fitness supply company. Danko earned his MBA at the University of Michigan and became dean at two leading American schools of business, Dartmouth and Villanova. He credits O'Toole's leadership insights with helping him lead with humility.

To be effective, O'Toole writes, leaders must begin by setting aside the culturally conditioned instinct to lead by pushing others and lead instead by the unnatural pull of inspiring values. He says that effective leadership will involve inspiring, lasting values of vision, trust, listening, authenticity, integrity, hope, and addressing the true needs of followers. O'Toole uses the example of Jesus as a leader when he writes:

> Can we imagine a situation where Jesus would be successful in winning over the crowd by being tough, abusive, and unconcerned about their needs?...Clearly the leadership of change does not depend on circumstances; it depends on the attitudes, values, and actions of leaders....The ultimate measure of Christ's leadership is that the movement he founded continued to spread after his death. In fact, from the

moment of his first conversions, Christianity belonged not to
Jesus but to the Christians.[1]

O'Toole maintains that only values-based leaders ultimately create organizations and followers who make a
long-lasting, positive impact in the world.

Leading from a core of eternal spiritual values is the
most effective and life-giving way to lead in sports or in
business, according to former NFL coach Tony Dungy.
After coaching the Indianapolis Colts to a Super Bowl
championship in 2007, Coach Dungy turned his attention
to writing books that lift up values leading to a life of significance. In his book *Uncommon*, Coach Dungy says that
the primary job of a coach is to build individuals who are
worthy of being role models—people of character, integrity, and courage, who have both confidence and humility.
Coach Dungy writes about confidence and humility:

> Born in humility, confidence is a recognition that life is not
> about me but about using the gifts and abilities I have been
> blessed with to their fullest. And it's not just using the gifts to
> benefit me, but to help my team and impact others. I appreci-
> ate that form of humility; it's not false modesty claiming that
> what you accomplished isn't important, but a realization that
> God created all of us with unique gifts and abilities. It's a
> different dynamic than tearing myself down; rather, it's try-
> ing to lift others up.[2]

Dungy's brother-in-law Loren tells a story in *Uncommon* of how Dungy models humility in his personal life.
When Dungy was coach of the Tampa Bay Buccaneers,
he invited Loren to a home game. The two men were to

share a room together in the team hotel the night before a big game. After dinner, Tony went up to bed while Loren stayed downstairs getting to know some of the professional football players he admired. When Loren retired to the hotel room, he discovered Tony asleep on the pull-out bed in the living room of the suite. The coach had left the bed in the bedroom for his brother-in-law to sleep in—the night before a big game. He realized that it was Tony's way of thinking about the well-being of others before himself.

The supreme model of humility is Jesus Christ himself. On the last night of his life here on earth, Jesus had a final meal with his followers. During that meal, Jesus got up from the table, tied a towel around himself, filled a bowl with water and knelt down before each of his disciples and washed and dried their feet. In the first century, everyone wore open-toed sandals as they walked the dusty roads of Palestine. Customarily, when people entered a home for dinner, a servant or a young child would kneel down and wash their feet before dinner. It was a humble task usually performed by someone other than the leader or the head of the household. However, Jesus wanted his disciples to realize that the humble service for others was to be the way of life for his followers, so he modeled humble service in a way that they could never forget. After washing and drying his followers' feet, Jesus gave them specific instructions that they should do the same. He said: "So if I, your Lord and teacher, have washed your feet, you too must wash each other's feet. I have given you an example: just as I have done, you also must do" (John 13:14-15).

Coach Brad Stevens and the Butler Bulldogs basketball team demonstrate humility in serving each other. Jesus also demonstrated the virtue of humility when he took a young child, put him in the midst of the disciples and said to them, "I assure you that if you don't turn your lives around and become like this little child, you will definitely not enter the kingdom of heaven. Those who humble themselves like this little child will be the greatest in the kingdom of heaven" (Matt. 18:3-4).

Furthermore, Jesus contrasted the ways of arrogant leaders who seek the spotlight for themselves with those who would follow him by saying, "But the one who is greatest among you will be your servant. All who lift themselves up will be brought low. But all who make themselves low will be lifted up" (Matt. 23:11-12).

Butler University basketball players are encouraged to live lives of humble service to each other, to their team, and to their community. Players who incorporate this value in their lives become not only successful on the basketball court but, more important, successful in the game of life.

A Humility Story

Ron Nored was an all-state point guard at Homewood High School in Homewood, Alabama. At Butler, Ron studied education and prepared to be an elementary school teacher. His own teachers and coaches had inspired Ron to cultivate the heart of an educator. One of the most important mentors and examples of education as a vocation of service was Ron's father. The Reverend Ron Nored Sr. was the full-time pastor in the African Methodist Episcopal Church and in addition taught seminary courses. It was through ministry to the people in the impoverished Birmingham, Alabama, neighborhood where the church is located that the elder Nored taught his son to serve others. In October 2003, when Ron Jr. was thirteen, his father died of cancer, but he left a deep impression on his son of the importance of living a life of humble service to others.

"I came to Butler to be a teacher. I had amazing teachers and coaches all my life, but my father was the most important teacher. When he passed away, it was a profound moment, for me, to step into a bigger role in the world, to set about becoming the teacher I was meant to be," Ron said. "I love being with people, helping them strive to be their best, to do better. And at the center of that is the belief that we are all called to be humble servants in this lifetime."

Sometimes the lessons of humility are not always what we want to learn, however. When Ron was a sophomore at Butler in 2010, he was point guard on the starting five that went to the championship game against Duke. In 2011, however, in the middle of the season, Coach Stevens asked another player to be the starting point guard, sending Nored to sit on the bench as one of the first substitutes. When a player has been a starter on the team as a sophomore and that team played in the championship game, he might expect that he will be the starting point guard the next year. However, Ron Nored was not on the starting five in the 2010–2011 season. A more ego-driven player might have become upset and discouraged by what he considered to be a demotion, but it was not so with Ron Nored. He trusted the coach's decision.

Things were to change, however. "Coach and I had a conversation after we lost to Youngstown State in 2011. He told me we were going to start doing different things. 'You're coming off the bench. Are you okay with that?' he asked me. And I remember thinking, *Are you serious? Of course I am okay with that.* I know those decisions have to be made. I signed up to be the best teammate I could be. I did not sign up to be a star. Since day one at Butler, Coach has been teaching us about humility and team and service. I knew that when it was my time to come off the bench I would make my contribution. I trusted Coach when he was starting me. How could I not trust him now?"

And that is where the principles of The Butler Way— and its foundational lesson in humility—can reflect a belief in the transcendent. For people of Christian faith it is an invitation to patience and steadfastness in times of loss as well as triumph. Jesus put it this way: "Happy are people who are humble, because they will inherit the earth" (Matt. 5:5).

PASSION

Nothing great in the world has been accomplished without passion.
—G. W. F. Hegel

Every great and commanding moment... is the triumph of some enthusiasm.
—Ralph Waldo Emerson

Don't you know that all the runners in the stadium run, but only one gets the prize? So run to win.
—Paul of Tarsus (1 Cor. 9:24)

"The kingdom of God is not coming with signs to be observed... for behold, the kingdom of God is in the midst of you."
—Jesus (Luke 17:20-21 RSV)

O God, help us to become masters of ourselves that we might be the servants of others. Take our minds and think through them, take our lips and speak through them and take our hearts and set them on fire. Amen.
—John Wesley

Ron Nored is described by his teammates on the Butler basketball team as "passionate," "enthusiastic," "excited," and "always on fire." He is the player who is seemingly always talking on the court, encouraging his teammates. In the locker room after a game, he is the one who leads the celebration when the team wins and the one who gives words of encouragement to other players after a loss.

Coach Stevens led the Butler Bulldogs to their second NCAA championship game in April 2011, against the University of Connecticut. The Butler team did not play with their usual scoring effectiveness and lost to U Conn by twelve points. After the game the Butler players went to the locker room discouraged and disappointed in themselves and their performance on the court. Dan Wetzel, a Yahoo! sports reporter, described what happened in the Butler dressing room after the team's disappointing loss.

> Butler player Shawn Vanzant sat in the corner of the room, sobbing and blaming himself for missing shots that might have turned the game around. Near him was star player Matt Howard, a towel over his head and tears streaming down his cheeks as he blamed himself for the loss. Rod Nored, red-eyed and tearful, made his way to Shawn Vanzant, pulled him up off his stool and hugged him. Then he hugged Matt Howard. Soon, all the players were standing up, hugging each other, crying and expressing their love for one another. In the midst of their pain, they loved and supported each other, rather than blaming another for the loss.

Later, Ron was asked why he started that hug fest in the locker room. He said, "That's why we're here—we're here for each other. In the big picture it is just a basketball game. It is really about the guys in this locker room. I wanted Shawn to know that we don't really care that his shot didn't go in; we care about him."[1]

In the midst of losing one of the biggest games in their lives, Nored helped his teammates understand that he is passionate not only about the game of basketball but, more important, about supporting his teammates as cherished friends, whether they win or lose. It is one thing to be committed to excellence during athletic training and within the competition of a game. It is another element of passion altogether that brings about the human connection. For Ron Nored it was an automatic response, the living out of a commitment he had long been devoted to. As the son of a pastor he has been taught from early childhood that friendship and community are at the center of a faithful life. He could not have responded any other way in the wake of the big loss at the Final Four.

"It is interesting how that moment has made an impression on people. At that time, it was just an automatic response for me. I saw the hurt in my teammates. I was hurting too. At that moment they were way more important than anything I was dealing with. I really just wanted to be there for them," he said. "So many people had been there for me when I had been at my worst, when I was down."

Passion Is Depth of Character

The true character of a person is revealed not when things are going well, but when things are not going well.

It is easy to be positive and encouraging when the team is winning or when everything is humming along pleasantly in our lives. However, true character emerges when we experience defeat and disappointment. The Butler basketball team players showed the depth of their character most clearly when they lost the 2011 NCAA championship game.

One team was celebrating their championship victory on the court with thousands of cheering fans and millions watching on television. The other team's members were supporting each other in their loss and saying things like "We're here for each other." "In the big picture it is just a basketball game." "I wanted Shawn to know that we don't really care that his shot didn't go in; we care about him."

Their words don't mean that the Butler players didn't want to win the game. They wanted to win with all their hearts. But in defeat they discovered that their passion and commitment to each other was a deeper and everlasting value. Victories in basketball and life may come and go, but the losing team's locker room held a lesson about eternal values that will last in the hearts and minds of those student athletes. The truth is that everyone experiences times of victory and defeat in their lives. Persons of character can experience victory without arrogance and defeat without despair.

Coach Stevens says the Rudyard Kipling poem "If" has had a profound impact on his approach to life and has helped shape his values and character. Here are some key lines from the poem:

If you can keep your head when all about you
Are losing theirs and blaming it on you,
If you can trust yourself when all men doubt you,
But make allowance for their doubting too;...

If you can meet with Triumph and Disaster
And treat those two imposters just the same;...

If you can force your heart and nerve and sinew
To serve your turn long after they are gone,
And so hold on when there is nothing in you
Except the Will which says to them: "Hold on!"...

If you can fill the unforgiving minute
With sixty seconds' worth of distance run,
Yours is the Earth and everything that's in it,
And—which is more—you'll be a Man, my son![2]

Everyone experiences times of disappointment and discouragement in their lives—these are the times that test our passion, enthusiasm, and commitment to our task and to each other.

The Source of Passion

What is the source of this power and passion?

Pharisees asked Jesus when God's kingdom was coming. He replied, "God's kingdom isn't coming with signs that are easily noticed. Nor will people say, 'Look, here it is!' or 'There it is!' Don't you see? God's kingdom is already among you." (Luke 17:20-21)

While other religious leaders looked for God's power and presence in outward signs, Jesus told them to look for the power and presence of God within themselves. It is as if God has created each person with God's passion and power within them. In a similar way, we are told in the first creation story in Genesis that

God created humanity
in God's own image,
in the divine image God created them,
male and female God created them (Gen. 1:27)

Jesus tells us that the power of God is within us, and God tells us in Genesis that we are all created in the image of God. This means that God's power, spirit, and image dwell in the hearts of every human being. The reflection of God within us is the source of our God-given passion and energy to make a positive difference in our lives and in our world.

A goal of life is to discover our God-given passion or enthusiasm, fan it into flame, and allow God to set our hearts on fire to enlighten and inspire all those around us.

The Greek roots of the word "enthusiasm" are *en* and *theos*, which means *in God* or *God in us*. When someone is enthusiastic or passionate, they have discovered the energetic power of God within them, motivating them to make a positive difference in the world. God is literally in them.

Author Marianne Williamson once wrote these words about the light and passion in every person:

You are a child of God. Your playing small does not serve the world....We are all meant to shine, as children do. We were born to make manifest the glory of God that is within us. It's not just in some of us; it's in everyone. And as we let our own light shine, we unconsciously give other people permission to do the same.[3]

Leading with Passion

Purpose, or vision, is the steering wheel, pointing the car in the right direction. But passion is the engine that makes it go. A vehicle functions best when the engine is running well and providing the energy needed to move forward and the steering wheel is pointed in the direction of the destination. Passion without vision is like a car with an engine but no steering wheel. We may generate a lot of energy but just go around in circles because we have no clear sense of direction. If we have a steering wheel but no engine, we will be pointed in the right direction, but we won't ever get there because we have no power or energy to move us forward.

The Butler University basketball team has players with the vision of playing well together as a team and the passion, enthusiasm, and energy to move the team forward—it's a powerful combination. Purpose comes from our head while passion comes from our heart. A person with a strong sense of purpose makes a mental commitment and says, "I will do this."

When people have a strong sense of purpose and also a heartfelt passion, not only do they reach their goal, but they set everyone around them on fire in the process.

Coach Stevens recruits players who have a commitment to play basketball with passion, enthusiasm, and excellence. He said one of the ways he can tell when a player has a passion for basketball is the response to a loss. After the game is over, when everyone else is gone, Coach Stevens often sees a player go back on the court to practice his shots and moves. When the coach sees that kind of response to a loss, he knows he has a player who has passion and commitment for the game and is on fire to improve himself as a basketball player.

Butler's Barry Collier says that passion means that players should not be lukewarm in their attitude and commitment but have a burning desire to play basketball to the best of their ability. He says that he can tell if a player is lukewarm or on fire to play basketball by simply watching how they move on the court. Players who are lukewarm seem to move without intention or purpose, but just by habit. When players are not fully present in the game or it seems as though their mind and thoughts are someplace else, they are lukewarm in their attitude and performance. But when a player is fully attentive, present, and engaged in the game, it will show by the intensity of their actions on the court.

As athletic director at Butler, Collier has strived to help all Butler coaches and all students regardless of gender or sport learn and live The Butler Way. So the culture of recruiting high-achieving students who have passion for their game, whatever the sport may be, is at the heart of athletics across the Butler campus. For women basketball players there may be no better reflection of this than Coach Beth Couture. When she arrived at Butler in 2002, Couture had inherited a demoralized team that finished the previous season with a record of 3-26. By the end of the 2009–2010 season, she had achieved 125 Butler career wins. It was the same year Couture battled and beat breast cancer, an experience that both tested her passion for the game and saw the game sustain her.

Couture learned she had cancer when in spring 2009 doctors discovered trouble during a routine physical. Earlier that year, she was reveling in the fact that her team had entered postseason tournament play. She felt fine and, at age forty-six, was in excellent physical condition, leading the stressful, but fulfilling, life of a college coach. "We had had a great season, and here I was with this cancer diagnosis. It was time to get into serious fight mode, to rely on all the lessons that athletics had taught me my whole life," she recalled. But this time, after more than twenty-five years as a coach, she was returning to the role of team player. Her teammates were surgeons, oncologists, radiologists, nurses, and fellow breast cancer patients. "I had to allow them to be my team," recalls Couture in the southern drawl of the South Carolina of her childhood. "In my passion for athletics all these years I had learned to face the challenges and adjust and adapt, and here I was getting the chance to do that because of cancer."

When Couture and her assistant coaches recruit students and work with the current roster of young women, they see their job as stoking the passion that players bring to the court, while teaching them the skills to be successful human beings no matter where life will take them. None of her players will taste the kind of fame that is possible for men in college basketball. Even the successful women players who see the victory of a Women's Final Four tournament or play in the WNBA will always need to have a special commitment to the personal passion of the game. But passion will sustain them no matter where life leads them.

"From day one in this program, we talk about how passion is foundational to who we are as a community," Couture explains. "If you are passionate about what you do, and follow that up with commitment to team, the constant practice of service and gratitude and humility, you will always be successful. That is because success will be measured by the content of who you are, who you are on the inside. We have to recruit for passion, because I cannot teach that. They have to bring that and a desire to be part of something bigger than their own life."

Collier says that each player's attitude affects the other players on the team. If a player is on fire — energetic and passionate — it will rub off on the other players on the team. Conversely, if a player is pessimistic and negative, it also rubs off on the rest of the team. This is why Butler coaches recruit passionate and enthusiastic players and seek to model passion, enthusiasm, and commitment themselves.

Collier also maintains that a player's commitment to excellence reveals passion. When players are committed to excellence, they constantly study tapes of the team's performance in previous games to see how they might improve their attitudes and actions on the court. When they are committed to excellence, they watch and study players who are better than they are so they might learn to improve themselves. Players committed to excellence are always open to their coach's instructions on improvement and are not defensive when the coach makes a suggestion to improve their performance.

In Scripture, Paul refers to rekindling passion into flame when he writes to his young friend Timothy: "Because of this, I'm reminding you to revive God's gift that is in you through the laying on of my hands. God didn't give us a spirit that is timid but one that is powerful, loving, and self-controlled" (2 Tim. 1:6-7).

Effective coaches and leaders in all areas of life are not only passionate themselves but also seek to rekindle into flame the passion in the hearts of the players on their team. For many people, the natural passion and enthusiasm in their hearts has been squashed by the experiences of life. They may have a burning desire to develop some area of their lives, but they have been told constantly that they can't do it. It's unfortunate, but teachers, family members and friends can discourage students from fanning into flame the embers of passion that smolder in their hearts. These well-meaning but misguided voices don't want their students to set unrealistic expectations or to shoot for more than they can accomplish, and tend to temper a student's enthusiasm. Good coaches and mentors help each player fan into flame the passionate commitment to become a better athlete, musician, teacher, scientist, businessman or woman, pastor, or any other role in life. Coach Stevens helps players uncover their passion, develop their abilities, and play with great enthusiasm and commitment.

At the beginning of a recent basketball season, Coach Stevens had six freshmen on his fifteen-player team roster. At one of the early season games, one of the freshmen played an outstanding game with significant scoring and rebounding. After the game was over, the opposing coach said to an assistant coach, "I thought we scouted that Butler player who played so well tonight. Why don't we have him on our team?" The assistant coach said, "He didn't play with all that enthusiasm and skill when we scouted him last year." Perhaps Coach Stevens and his assistant coaches could smell the smoke of the burning passion in their freshman player, and they fanned it into flame. Our passion for basketball and life also reveals the depth of our commitment to the tasks ahead of us. An anonymous author wrote these words about commitment:

Commitment is what transforms a promise into reality.
It is the words that speak boldly of your intentions.
And the actions which speak louder than words.

It is making the time where there is none:
Coming through time after time; year after year.

Commitment is the stuff character is made of;
The power to change the face of things.
It is the daily triumph of integrity over skepticism.

Many young people display great promise. They have the potential to become outstanding athletes, musicians, and scholars, or to excel in numerous other fields. However, people who have great promise or potential but who lack a corresponding depth of commitment and passion rarely fulfill their potential.

Commitment is what transforms a promise into reality.

A Story of Passion

Coach Stevens refers to Butler player Matt Howard as one of the most committed players he has ever coached. He says Howard is one of Butler's best four-year players, and it's because of Howard's total commitment at every practice and every game.

Matt Howard is the eighth of ten children born to Stan and Linda Howard. Matt grew up in a three-bedroom home in rural Connersville, population 14,800, about fifty miles southeast of Indianapolis. His father works for the U.S. Postal Service and has taken one sick day in thirty-three years as a mail carrier. Matt began delivering the Connersville *News Examiner* at age nine, learning early the value of regular commitment and hard work. Matt also learned from his large family the value of cooperating with others to achieve your goals.

At six foot seven, Matt was an outstanding Connersville high school basketball player, and he received numerous awards during his high school basketball career. Matt's high school coach Rodney Klein was even heard to say that Matt shows that if you work hard and do things the right way, you will be rewarded for it.

Coach Stevens recruited Matt Howard to play for the Butler bulldogs in 2007. As a freshman, Howard was the Horizon League newcomer of the year and played a prominent role in the Bulldogs' first-round victory over South Alabama in the 2008 NCAA tournament. As a junior at Butler, Howard helped the 2009–2010 Bulldogs make it to the NCAA championship game. As a senior in 2011, Howard scored a tip-in as the time expired to defeat Old Dominion in the second round NCAA tournament game. Then in the third round of the tournament, he made the winning free throw with 0.8 seconds left to clinch a 71-70 victory over the number one–seeded Pittsburgh Panthers. Matt Howard was one of the reasons that Butler played in the NCAA final four games in both 2010 and 2011.

Howard also earned Academic All-American honors in 2009, 2010, and 2011. He was named the 2011 Men's Basketball Academic All-American of the year. He graduated with a grade point average of 3.77, with a major in finance. Following his graduation from Butler, Matt Howard signed to play professional basketball with the Olympiacos of the Greek League.

Coach Stevens once said about Matt Howard, "Matt

sets a tone of unselfishness with everything he does." Noted sports reporter Rick Reilly said that Howard "looks more like a geeky band camp resident assistant than a possible NBA first rounder." Reilly went on to describe Howard:

> The Bulldogs wouldn't be anywhere near Houston without Howard. He's the designated floor diver, the insatiable rebounder, the guy who sets the kind of picks that would stop an Amtrak train....He's the thing you love most in a college basketball player—a guy who just wants to win and doesn't care who gets the credit. A guy who hits class by day and glass by night. A scabbed-knee grinder who finishes every game with his tank on E.[4]

Coach Stevens said that Matt Howard only had one speed on the court and that was full speed ahead, all the time—an embodiment of The Butler Way.

Howard has been known for his eccentricities, both on and off the court. His teammate Shelvin Mack told Reilly that Howard had six pairs of new shoes in his locker but refused to wear them, preferring to stay with what Mack described as "ratty old ones." Howard also habitually rode a rusted-out bicycle to Butler's 6 a.m. practices, regardless of the weather. During one 2011 ice storm, the handlebars bent under him while he was riding, causing him to fall on the ice. He would say about this incident, "I fixed it. Just poured some WD-40 in there and bent them back. It's a little risky to ride, I guess, but I can't see buying a new one."

Matt Howard was deeply admired and appreciated by

Butler fans and his teammates for his passion for basketball, his scrappy commitment, and his determined hard work, which have enabled him to be one of the few players from Butler to make it into the professional basketball circuit. In the Butler men's basketball locker room, Coach Stevens has placed a sign with PASSIONATE written in large letters followed by the words: "About Butler University, his team, and this program." Every time a player, coach, or visitor walks into that locker room, they are met with those words to remind them to bring their heartfelt passion and commitment to everything they do at Butler University.

The whiteboard behind Stevens's desk reads, "Intentional commitment to be consistently present." Coach Stevens knows that players must be present if they are to play with passion and enthusiasm. If players focus their attention on mistakes they have made in the past or on fear about missing a shot in the future, they will fail to be fully present and effective in the current moment.

The current moment is the only moment anyone ever has. The past is gone and the future is not here, so the only moment we ever have to live is the present moment. When we are not fully present and passionate about this moment of life, we miss an opportunity to live fully and completely. Coach Stevens sometimes uses a time-out in a game to get his players to let go of whatever shots have been missed or mistakes made in the past few minutes and to focus their attention totally and completely on the current moment and what needs to be done now to win the game.

When a time-out is called, the players gather around their coach with their full and complete attention. Observers often wonder what the coach said in that brief time-out, but what he said may not be as important as what he does in helping them focus their attention and commitment on the current moment in the game.

It's a lesson for us all: we cannot ever be passionate about life when our minds and our attention are someplace else rather than focused on the only time God has given us to live, which is the present.

Perhaps that is why the Psalms give us the reminder: "This is the day that the LORD has made; / let us rejoice and be glad in it" (Ps. 118:24 NRSV). The present moment is the only moment we ever have to practice passion and commitment and to discover, as the athletes at Butler have, that finding and developing passion is what makes the game worth playing.

UNITY

*Individual commitment to a group effort—that is what makes a team
work, a company work, a society work, a civilization work.*
—Vince Lombardi

*Getting good players is easy. Getting them to play together is
the hard part.*
—Casey Stengel

T.E.A.M. means Together Everyone Achieves More.
—Author unknown

*But God has so arranged the body . . . that there may be no dissension
within the body, but the members may have the same care
for one another.*
—Paul of Tarsus (1 Cor. 12:24b-25 NRSV)

*And when day came, he called his disciples and chose twelve of them,
whom he also named apostles.*
—Jesus (Luke 6:13 NRSV)

During one preseason practice, Coach Stevens asked
one of his assistant coaches to record the time it took each

player to run what are called "suicide drills." This drill is a speed and conditioning exercise where a player starts at the baseline at one end of the basketball court and runs as fast as he can to the free-throw line and back to the baseline. Then he runs from the baseline to the half court line and back. Then he runs to the free-throw line at the opposite end of the court and back. Finally he runs to the baseline at the far end of the court and back to the starting baseline.

Coach Stevens told each player to run four "suicide drills." They would be timed on each one. The players assumed that they would be evaluated on how fast they could complete it.

When the exercise was over, players' performance statistics were given to Coach Stevens. He stood before the exhausted players and threw the sheets on the floor. Coach Stevens said, "I don't really care how fast you can run 'suicide drills.' I did this exercise to see if any of you would encourage another player to improve their time on the 'suicide drill.' Only two of you did it. Only two of the fourteen players here encouraged another player while they were running this exercise."

The coach explained that one of the core values of the Butler team is unity, or teamwork. During the season, the players need to remember that it is not only about how well each of them play individually but about how well each player encourages his teammates to do their best in a game. When everyone encourages and supports one another, they all play better basketball and are a better team.

Coach Stevens often invites Butler University staff and fans to attend closed preseason practice sessions. Observers are often surprised that whenever a player falls to the floor in the midst of a vigorous scrimmage, all the players on the team (including those on the bench) run to the fallen player to support him. If one of the players falls and another player does not run to help him, the head coach will ask that player why he doesn't care about his fallen teammate.

During an in-season basketball game, if a Butler player falls to the floor during the game, every Butler player on the court will be at his side in seconds. Coach Stevens develops teamwork and unity on his team by encouraging every player to be concerned about the well-being of his teammates.

At Butler basketball games, whenever a player is replaced on the court and returns to the bench, all the other players on the bench stand up and acknowledge that player for his contribution to the team, regardless of how well he has done at any particular moment. Every player is spoken to and welcomed when he comes off the court by the coaches and all the players on the bench. This practice dramatically contrasts with the way players on other teams are often treated when they return to the bench, unnoticed or acknowledged by their teammates, as if they are unimportant now that they are off the court.

These practices are some of the ways Stevens strives to instill unity. Through these rituals of connection and interdependence, he teaches players to support and care for each other as teammates.

Jan Stevens, Brad Stevens's mother, says that Brad, an only child, has always loved to work with teams of people. When he was a little boy growing up in Zionsville, Indiana, the Stevens home was always filled with neighborhood kids. "On any given day, after school or on the weekends, there were always lots of his friends with us. There was a game going. I made sure there were plenty of snacks for everyone," Jan Stevens recalls. "It was the way it always was." And Brad Stevens loved it.

As a child, Brad had a basketball hoop in his driveway. Every day he would go out and shoot hoops and, within minutes, four or five neighborhood boys would be on his driveway for a basketball game. When the weather was bad and Brad and his friends couldn't play outside, he would ask his parents to take them to an indoor court downtown where they could play basketball together. Brad was usually the team leader in organizing their neighborhood basketball games, and his teammates were his best friends. At the center of his athletic life were team sports—in addition to basketball, there was soccer and baseball. Stevens was never interested in individual sports, such as track or tennis or golf. He relished the chance to be part of a team.

The commitment paid off when, during junior and senior high school, Stevens had become good enough to snag an invitation to the American Athletic Union team. It's a program for the best of young players and Steven's team won national honors several times. On the AAU team, he got to know and love players from a wide variety of social and economic backgrounds. He frequently brought all of his AAU buddies to his home after games for food and fellowship. Playing on these teams taught Brad to disregard culture and ethnicity. As a coach, Stevens looks for players on his team who are willing to practice the values of humility, passion, unity, service, thankfulness, and accountability, regardless of who they are or where they are from.

One of the reasons Stevens chose DePauw University in Greencastle, Indiana, for his undergraduate degree was that many of his friends from Zionsville went to DePauw. In fact, fourteen from his high school community went to DePauw University when Stevens was a student there. He is energized when he is with others and inspired to be part of a team and to be truly connected to the players and assistant coaches he leads. Yet time alone is essential to his work and life. Frequently the coach wakes up early—often at or before dawn—so that he can have time for silence. He is known to arrive early at Hinkle Fieldhouse, the legendary home to Butler athletics, and be the first one to unlock the doors to the basketball program offices. Characteristically, an hour or two before a game, Stevens wraps up meetings, court time, and conversations with players or assistants. He may turn off his phone and log off his computer. This is his time to read from the Scriptures or to simply be quiet. "I know that I am someone who needs to be prepared and when that is done, it is done. Then I need time to think and time for some quiet," Stevens said. It is an essential part of his commitment to others as a leader to make time for himself in silence and solitude.

On Coach Stevens's desk in the head coach's office at Hinkle Fieldhouse is a well-worn copy of *The Coach's Bible*, which Brad received from the Fellowship of Christian Athletes. About an hour before every game, Coach Stevens goes into his office for a quiet time of reading and reflection. During that time, he reads scriptures from *The Coach's Bible* or from other inspirational writings to get his mind off the pressure of the coming game and to focus on eternal values and virtues. Some of the Scripture texts that Stevens has found helpful are:

> Do not be conformed to this age, but be transformed by the renewing of your mind, so that you may discern what is the good, pleasing, and perfect will of God. (Rom. 12:2 HCSB)

> But seek first the kingdom of God and His righteousness, and all these things will be provided for you. Therefore don't worry about tomorrow, because tomorrow will worry about itself. Each day has enough trouble of its own. (Matt. 6:33-34 HCSB)

> I am able to do all things through Him who strengthens me. (Phil. 4:13 HCSB)

> So then, we must pursue what promotes peace and what builds up one another. (Rom. 14:19 HCSB)

To build team unity and spirit, Tracy Stevens hosts the basketball team, assistant coaches, and their families once a month. The players love to come for a home-cooked meal that she and the wives of the assistant coaches provide, and they appreciate the opportunity to get away from the pressures of college and basketball. With all the coaches' families present, they see their coaches as good husbands to their wives and fathers to their children. Some of the athletes grew up with single moms, so it is especially helpful for them to experience good male role models of loving and caring husbands and fathers. "The experience has helped me see Coach Stevens as a model for me, not only as a coach and teacher, but as a man," said Ron Nored.

By the end of the basketball season, the coaches, their wives and families, and all of the players on the team have become an extended family where each one knows and cares about the others as persons and not simply as basketball players or coaches. Such work at building unity doesn't go unnoticed. Sportswriters often comment on the level of teamwork and unity within the Butler University team. Noted sports reporter Dick Vitale wrote, "If you want to learn how basketball is played in its purest form—the team game—learn all you can about Butler hoops. They represent what college basketball is all about."[1]

Butler University may not always have the most outstanding individual players in the nation, but they have a system of values that emphasizes teamwork and enables them to play highly effective basketball against highly touted individual players. "We do not recruit the kind of player who plans to be a star or who sees his role as strictly the stand-out player. That is just not the kind of program we have. We are a team first, and we teach that from the moment we meet a potential recruit. It is a message we carry forward in the first weeks of the new (academic) year," Stevens said. "This is who we are."

Fellow Butler coach Beth Couture knows this fact, as well. Couture watches closely how her colleague teaches the concept, and she has watched it prove successful when the Butler Bulldogs win. "One way of understanding winning is that winning is always doing the right thing, and as a team we strive to win in those terms every day," Couture said. "But it is clear that we want to win games. And we teach our players that when we establish these values of team and unity, humility, service, passion and gratitude, we will win. But we win because of these values, not in spite of them."

One of Couture's greatest supporters is a woman athlete who never played for one of Couture's teams. Mary Shaw played point guard for Butler from 1989 to 1993. Back then there was no Butler Way. But there was a sense from the first day in Hinkle Fieldhouse that Butler and the women's team fostered a sense of family, Shaw said. There were no aphorisms on the locker room walls and no philosophy spelled out in the playbook. But there was a clear sense that the Butler players brought a commitment to work, to ethics, to personal best and, perhaps most of all, she said, to collaboration and teamwork. They had to, because it was never a program built on superstars.

"With Butler it was never ever about winning at all

costs," said Shaw. "In the college sports world where so much is about making money and building prestige, there is purity and an innocence. When I think back now on my Butler years, that is what I know to be true. You play at Butler to be part of a team, to be part of something bigger than yourself. It is about team, and I think it ends up being about love."

After majoring in marketing, Shaw went on to work for a marketing research firm and eventually opened her own sports marketing and silk-screening company. During the mid-2000s she was able to begin giving back to the university that had helped nurture her into adulthood when she began hosting players for meals in her home. She also holds fund-raising dinners to strengthen the profile—and stoke the passion—for women's athletics at Butler. "Athletics helped me grow up and become a disciplined person. It taught me how to lead a team in my business life. So I think I will always be grateful to the team I was part of as a student."

Reflecting on the astonishing, unimagined success of the back-to-back Final Four appearances of 2010 and 2011, Couture saw the men's team thrive above all because of unity. They worked together to win. "Our men are such a good example of how a team of reasonably talented players can beat a group of players who are taller and bigger and arguably have more talent. You watch our guys warm up against Ohio State (University) or Pitt (University of Pittsburgh) and you would think we have no chance. Athlete to athlete they are bigger, longer, quicker. But our guys help each other out. They believe in each other. And they win. Team will beat a group of individuals. I have seen it again and again. I believe it."

The Jesus Movement

At the beginning of his ministry, Jesus called together a team of followers, whom he called apostles.

During that time, Jesus went out to the mountain to pray, and he prayed to God all night long. At daybreak, he called together his disciples. He chose twelve of them whom he called apostles: Simon, whom he named Peter; his brother Andrew; James; John; Philip; Bartholomew; Matthew; Thomas; James the son of Alphaeus; Simon, who was called a zealot; Judas the son of James; and Judas Iscariot, who became a traitor. (Luke 6:12-16)

Why did Jesus choose to gather a team of close followers around him? Theoretically, as the Son of God, Jesus could have accomplished his mission alone. But he selected a motley group of twelve rather ordinary men as his team of choice. Jesus spent three years molding his team into faithful followers. It was to his twelve close friends, as well as many followers, that he gave what we call the Sermon on the Mount found in Matthew 5–7. It was the twelve who were witnesses when Jesus healed lepers, the blind, the lame, a bent-over woman, and a man with a withered hand. These twelve friends witnessed Jesus raise Lazarus from the dead. They traveled with him all over Galilee and Judea, listening to his teachings and asking him the questions—the same ones we all would have asked if we were there.

It was the team of twelve who were with him on the Sea of Galilee when the storm arose and they feared drowning, until he calmed the sea. And it was the team of twelve who saw him walk across the water to their boat in the night.

Later it was to the team of twelve Jesus gave authority to preach, teach, and heal. It was this team who were sent out to spread God's good news throughout Galilee. And it was the team of twelve who took the five loaves and two fish Jesus blessed, and fed five thousand men and an uncounted number of women and children.

It was the team of twelve who went into Jerusalem during the last week of his life and joined him in his last supper. It was the team of twelve who abandoned him as he hung on the cross and died. They were also the ones to whom the women brought the good news of his resurrection.

Finally, it was the team of twelve to whom the Holy Spirit came on Pentecost and who were filled with the spiritual power to proclaim the resurrection and living presence of Jesus and who were used by God to start and expand the Jesus movement throughout the world.

From the very beginning, the Jesus movement has been carried out through the team effort of these first followers of Jesus. Consequently, those who call themselves followers of Jesus today also become faithful team members with other followers in sharing God's Good News. St. Paul also emphasized the importance of teamwork when he described the church as the body of Christ:

> Christ is just like the human body—a body is a unit and has many parts; and all the parts of the body are one body, even though there are many. . . . But God has put the body together, giving greater honor to the part with less honor. . . . If one part suffers, all the parts suffer with it; if one part gets the glory, all the parts celebrate with it. (1 Cor. 12:12; 24b, 26)

Teamwork and unity characterize other religious traditions, as well. Great leaders gathered teams of followers around them to continue their message and ministry. Moses called a team of leaders to help him administer the affairs of the Hebrew people on their way from slavery in Egypt to freedom in Canaan. Mohammad had devoted followers who listened to his teachings and carried them on after his death. Devoted followers surround Buddhist, Hindu, and Sikh holy men and practice the teachings of their masters. Religious leaders from various traditions brought together followers who were called to work together for the sake of their particular mission.

Teamwork is not only a high value for basketball teams. It is a high value for people in many religious traditions, as well.

Why Do Geese Fly in a V Formation?

Every fall thousands of geese fly from Canada to the southern part of the United States to escape the bitterly cold Canadian winter. As soon as a flock of geese take flight from Canadian waters, they quickly form a V-shape flying pattern, with one goose in the center leading and all the other geese trailing behind in two close lines.

Wildlife scientists have conducted extensive studies to determine why geese and other migratory birds always fly in this distinctive V-formation. What they found is fascinating. One, they discovered that when geese fly together, each goose provides additional lift and reduces air resistance for the goose flying behind it. Consequently, scientists estimate that the whole flock, by flying together in a V-formation, can fly about 70 percent farther with the same amount of energy than if each goose flew alone. Geese have discovered that they can reach their destination more quickly and with less energy expended when they fly together in formation. When people work together harmoniously on teams, sharing common values and a common destination, they all arrive at the destination more quickly and easily because they are lifted up by one another's energy and enthusiasm.

Two, when a goose drops out of the V-formation, it quickly discovers that it requires a great deal more effort and energy to fly. Consequently, that goose will quickly return to the formation to take advantage of the lifting power that comes from flying together. Sometimes people playing on teams will drop out of the group and try to accomplish goals on their own. However, like the geese, they usually discover that they miss the synergy and energy that comes when they are an active part of a cohesive team moving toward their destination, and want to return to the group.

Three, geese rotate leadership. The goose flying in the front of the formation has to expend the most energy because it is the first to break up the flow of air to provide the additional lift for all of the geese who follow. When the lead goose gets tired, it drops out of the front position and moves to the rear of the formation, where the resistance is lightest, and another goose moves to the leadership position. This rotation of position happens many times in the course of the long journey to warmer climates. When a team is functioning well, various members of the team may take the leadership role for a while because of a particular expertise or experience. As a result, on good teams, everyone has the opportunity to serve as a leader as well as a follower.

Four, geese honk at each other. Geese frequently make loud honking sounds as they fly together. Scientists speculate that this honking is their way of communicating with each other during their long flight. Similarly, when working on teams, it is exceedingly important for each team member to communicate regularly with all the other team members. Teams frequently fall apart because of a lack of adequate communication among the various members of the team. Perhaps human teams can learn from flying flocks of geese that constant communication among members is exceedingly important in moving effectively toward a common destination.

Five, geese help each other. Scientists also discovered that when one goose becomes ill, is shot or injured, and drops out of the formation, two other geese will fall out of formation and remain with the weakened goose. They will stay with and protect the injured goose from predators until it is able to fly again or dies. Likewise, human teams work best when they do more than just work together, but when they care for the well-being of each other.

And what does The Butler Way have in common with geese? Just as geese provide mutual lift, Butler teammates provide lift for each other on the basketball court when they set picks and screens that enable another player to get an open shot. Players rotate leadership on the court in each game when they discover that one particular player is "hot" in hitting shots, and they help that person become the leading scorer in that game. The key to effective teamwork on the basketball court or in life is the constant communication among teammates that is essential to achieve a common goal. Coach Couture says about her teams, "A lot of times, when things go south, it is about relationships. This one thinks she should play. Or one player said another player yelled at her on the court. Guys confront this right on the spot and move on. Women have to talk it out. They have to express themselves, be heard, reconcile."

Finally, when one member of the team falls to the floor or is injured, each member of the Butler team rushes to help his fallen teammate. Synergy is sometimes defined as "one plus one equals more than two." When individuals work together as highly effective teams in sports, religion, business, health care, or any other pursuit, they discover a synergy that makes them all more effective in achieving higher goals than they could ever achieve alone.

Business Teams

During the past few decades, many American businesses have moved from a primarily authoritarian to a more team-oriented decision-making structure. More and more businesses are introducing teamwork as part of their organizational and production processes. Some business teams have produced exceptional results, while other teams have been counterproductive, depending on the makeup, mission, and cohesiveness of the team.

The purpose of business teams is to bring workers together in cohesive and cooperative groups of people to achieve a common goal. If teams are not cohesive and cooperative with each other, or they experience a great deal of interpersonal conflict, the team will usually fail to be productive. However, when the right people are put on the right team and given clear goals and instructions, the results of their work together usually exceed previous results and benefit the company and the people involved.

The Ford Motor Company moved from lagging sales and severe competition from foreign manufacturers to greater success by forming teams composed of individuals from various departments in the company. Ford executives decided on a new approach to producing the Ford Taurus automobile and formed a new group called Team Taurus. Team Taurus had representatives from all departments responsible for planning, designing, engineering, and manufacturing. This team had ultimate responsibility for designing the new automobile.

Advantages to the team approach became apparent immediately. Problems with the design of the new automobile were identified and corrected by all of the departments who would eventually have to engineer and manufacture the Taurus. Assembly workers were brought into the process, and made valuable suggestions on streamlining manufacturing steps for greater efficiency in construction and a higher quality automobile. For example, assembly line workers suggested that the number of parts in a door panel be reduced from eight to two for a more solid door and easier assembly.

The normal five-year process for the development and production of a new automobile was drastically reduced, and a more competitive American-made car was put on the market sooner than would be expected. The Ford Taurus has become one of the best-selling cars in America.

Southwest Airlines is another corporation that utilizes teamwork in its highly effective and profitable business. Jerome Schaum, a Southwest first officer, wrote about teamwork at Southwest:

> How can Southwest Airlines turn an airplane in twenty-five minutes? The answer is Teamwork. Ramp agents, fuelers, agents, mechanics, and service personnel swarm the airplane as soon as it parks at the gate. In the cabin, flight attendants clean each row of seats as soon as customers vacate them. In the terminal, the gate agents are helping more customers

check in while the operations agents are preparing to begin the boarding process. In the cockpit, the first officer is busy preparing the aircraft to fly to the next destination. Meanwhile, the captain is assisting in cleaning the cabin or aiding in the pre-boarding of customers with disabilities....Everyone is working and working hard....Of course it doesn't seem like work when you are having fun. There is satisfaction in knowing you are part of a team, a combined effort producing a greater result than any individual effort.[2]

These committed teams of workers who are willing to do what it takes, whether it is in their job description or not, have made Southwest Airlines one of the most popular and profitable airlines in America. Consider an operation where the captain is expected to help clean in order to achieve an on-time takeoff.

Players on the Butler University basketball team who adopt the value of teamwork and do whatever it takes to make the team successful are well prepared to go into businesses that have developed highly effective and productive teams.

Learning Teamwork from the Team

David Woods has been the *Indianapolis Star* beat writer for the Butler Bulldogs basketball team since 2001. In 2009 Woods wrote an article about how new Butler players learn the Butler system of play from older players:

Sophomore Matt Howard didn't learn Butler's style of basketball from the coaching staff. Older players took care of that. Former teammate Drew Streicher demonstrated every move and nuance. Howard said he became sick of listening to Julian Betko, another former teammate, except that Betko was always right. He just understood the Butler system so well, Howard said.[3]

Butler players who are committed to the team's basketball system are also committed to teaching the new players the system and incorporating them into the team. There are more signs and quotations in the Butler University men's locker room about team than about any other topic. One sign has these large letters:

TEAM FIRST: EMBRACES AND EXHIBITS THE ATTITUDE OF A GREAT TEAMMATE.

Another sign reads:

GREAT TEAMS HAVE GREAT TEAMMATES.

GREAT TEAMS DO DIFFICULT THINGS TOGETHER.

Another large sign has a quotation by a former player:

"The best thing about Butler is great teammates and that includes coaches. There is a proven system that works, and it involves everyone—the results over the last decade prove it." —Matt Howard

A quotation from Bill Bradley, former NBA great and former U.S. Senator from New Jersey, is also included on the team's locker room wall:

"Championship teams share a moment that few other people know. The overwhelming emotions are derived from more than pride. Your devotion to your teammates, the depth of your sense of belonging, is something like blood kinship....Rarely can words fully express it. It is the bond that selflessness forges." —Bill Bradley

These words written by former Butler coach Todd Lickliter also appear on a sign in the locker room:

To preserve the Butler way we will:

1. Place the well-being of our teammates before individual desires.

2. Embrace the process of growth.

3. Execute the Butler system.

4. Demonstrate toughness in every circumstance.

In Coach Stevens's office is a large sign on the wall behind his desk that contains a quotation from Don Mattingly, New York Yankee captain and All-Star first baseman:

Team sports are really difficult things. Sometimes your team wins because of you, sometimes in spite of you, and sometimes it's like you're not even there. That's the reality of the team game. At one point in my career something wonderful happened. I don't know why or how, but I came to understand what "team" meant. It meant that although I didn't get a hit or make a great defensive play, I could impact the team in an incredible and consistent way. I learned that I could impact my team by caring first and foremost about the team's success and not my own. I don't mean by rooting for us like a typical fan. I mean care, really care about the team, about "us." I became less selfish, less lazy,

less sensitive to negative comments. When I gave up "me"
I became more. I became a captain, a leader, a better person
and I came to understand that life is a "team game." I've
found that most people aren't team players. They don't realize that life is the only game in town. Someone should
tell them. It has made all the difference in the world to me.
—Don Mattingly

On the whiteboard behind his desk Coach Stevens has
written these phrases attributed to Don Meyer: "There is
nothing more harmful to your team than a lack of discipline." "Great team: everyone does the dirty jobs." "Every
team has to form its own culture too."

At the beginning of each season Stevens asks his players their definition of a great team and writes down all the
qualities they admire in a great team. Then he asks them
if they have ever played on a great team. Most have not
played on a team with all the qualities listed, so he enrolls
them in a vision of playing on a great team now by personally practicing the qualities they have already listed as
attributes of a great team. Also on the whiteboard behind
his desk Coach Stevens has written these words: "True
definition of team: Have you seen one?"

Stevens and his coaching staff emphasize the unity of
the team and teamwork more often than any of the other
principles because a basketball team is successful only
when the individual team members consistently care for
each other as persons and play well together. Any individual player can undermine the whole team by selfish or

negative actions. Players are reminded regularly: "Do not divide our team."

The Butler Way requires everyone to remember what Jesus said: "A kingdom involved in civil war will collapse. And a house torn apart by divisions will collapse" Mark 3:24.

chapter four

SERVANTHOOD

The best way to find yourself is to lose yourself in the service of others.
—Mohandas Gandhi

Service to others is the rent you pay for your room here on earth.
—Muhammad Ali

Servant leadership begins with the natural feeling that one wants to serve; to serve first. Then conscious choice brings one to aspire to lead.
—Robert K. Greenleaf

Whoever wants to be great among you will be your servant. Whoever wants to be first among you will be the slave of all, for the Human One didn't come to be served but rather to serve and to give his life to liberate many people.
—Jesus (Mark 10:43-45)

O Lord, Help us to become masters of ourselves that we might be the servants of others.
—John Wesley

Mark and Jan Stevens joined the Zionsville United Methodist Church in Zionsville, Indiana, when their son

Brad Stevens was nine years old. During his junior and senior high school years, Brad became active in the church youth group. It had a significant impact on his life. While in high school, Brad went on a work mission project to Mississippi and later on a work project to Texas with his church youth group. Decades later, from his coach's office at Hinkle Fieldhouse, Stevens talks about the impact of these mission trips on his life. Being with people who lived in great poverty and need inspired in him a desire to serve other people. He grew up in an affluent suburb of Indianapolis, but early on developed a deep compassion for people who do not have the same opportunities as he experienced in his family and community. "It became part of what I understood it meant to be in a community and to be a human being," Stevens said. "I want to do what I can to make service part of what these guys experience while they are here, while they are playing. It is not separated from that." He added that he considers it to be part of learning how to live an integrated life.

To teach this, Stevens and his staff serve people caught in the pain of poverty. They look for projects that are accessible and that fill a true local need, while helping students engage. Each year during the Christmas season, the Butler basketball team, through the Indianapolis United Christmas Service, adopts an Indianapolis area family in need—generally a large extended family with eight to twelve family members. The coaches receive the name, age, gender, and gift desires of each person in their adopted family. The basketball team is expected not only to buy warm clothes and toys on each list but also to provide food for the family. The basketball coaches' wives and family members go shopping and purchase Christmas gifts and food for each member of their adopted family. Brad and Tracy invite all of the basketball players, the assistant coaches, and the coaches' wives to their home where the players have the assignment to wrap all the Christmas gifts for the family they have decided to serve that year. After the presents are all wrapped, the coaches and players personally deliver the gifts to the family they are serving.

Some of the players come from affluent homes and may not necessarily be aware of the needs of low-income families in their communities. Some of the players come from low-income families and are well aware of the value of these Christmas gifts to people in need. Regardless of their backgrounds, all of the players see the model of the coaches and their families spending their own money and taking their own time to help provide Christmas gifts for families in need. It is a simple exercise—giving time and financial resources at Christmas to help others.

It's an exercise that many of the players, like many other Butler students, are familiar with, since this is a generation of young people who have grown up with the concept of service to others. They learned as early as grade school that service projects are part of an education, part of growing up, and the stuff of resumes and college applications. However, there is something much more important being practiced at Butler. The players and their coaches are pulling away from the pressures and stress of an academic semester and the start of a basketball season to be part of something bigger. They are being given a chance to lose a little bit of themselves as they give to others. They are called to give here, so they can give to their teammates back on the court. And they are called not only to keep in perspective and balance the importance of their sport but also the importance of their academic work and their life beyond Butler.

A few times each season, members of the basketball team work at the soup kitchen at North United Methodist Church, a congregation less than two miles from the serene, bucolic Butler campus. North Church is located at a kind of social and economic crossroads in the center of Indianapolis. To the north of the church is Butler and the lovely homes of middle-class and wealthy people. To the south are high-density, low-income apartment buildings. People enter this church from both sides, coming together to form congregation, community, and a family of faith. North is also known as a place where community dinners flip the script: the people who cannot afford dinner help serve it alongside people who have helped buy the food. People who helped buy the food sit beside the poorest church members to be served and to be in fellowship. Butler players, in the midst of their basketball season, come to North Church to serve low-income and homeless families a hot meal during the cold winter. And in turn, they are called to grow in gratitude, as well as in the capacity to serve beyond themselves.

Coach Stevens learned servanthood when he was a

college student. Even though he had experienced mission trips and local church-based service projects, true formation in servant leadership didn't begin in full until Stevens was a student at DePauw University in Greencastle, Indiana. There, he worked as an intern at the Hartman Center for Civic Education and Leadership, the campus center where students engage in service as a way of becoming better citizens and leaders. During the internship he studied the work of Robert K. Greenleaf, the leading twentieth-century proponent of the servant as leader, and the person who shaped a philosophy of leadership rooted in the care of others first. In his essay "The Servant as Leader," Greenleaf wrote that servant leaders recognize their responsibility to contribute to the well-being of people in their community and world:

> [Servant Leadership] begins with the natural feeling that one wants to serve, to serve *first*. Then conscious choice brings one to aspire to lead. That person is sharply different from one who is *leader* first, perhaps because of the need to assuage an unusual power drive or to acquire material possessions....The leader-first and the servant-first are two extreme types. Between them there are shadings and blends that are part of the infinite variety of human nature.[1]

Larry Spears, who served as president and CEO of the Robert K. Greenleaf Center for Servant Leadership in Indianapolis from 1990 to 2007, said there are ten characteristics that are central to the development of a servant leader. They are listening, empathy, healing, awareness, persuasion, conceptualization, foresight, stewardship, commitment to the growth of people, and building community.

The Butler University athletic department cites "servanthood" as a key principle because it focuses on building leaders who see themselves first of all as servants. Basketball players are taught servanthood through the phrase "make your teammates better, lead by giving." Butler basketball coaches see themselves first as servants to the players they coach. The question they ask themselves is, "How can I help this player grow and develop as a person and as a player?" rather than, "How can I make this player do what I want him or her to do?"

Their focus is on the growth and development of each player rather than on how they can simply use any particular player to increase their number of winning games during the season.

Because the coaches model and teach servanthood, the players see themselves as servants of each other. Their goal is to serve each other in such a way that the whole team improves and succeeds.

Players often become famous and honored for the number of points they score in a game. However, before any player can score points, another player has to assist by throwing that player the basketball. The Butler basketball coaches keep close track not only of who scores the most points in a game but also of who gives the most "assists." Players who give "assists" are honored along with the players who score the most points in any particular game. In this way, players are taught the value of assisting and serving each other rather than simply thinking about their own personal record of points scored in a game or in a season.

Another one of the signs Coach Stevens has posted in the Butler locker room reads: "SERVICE: FOCUS ON LIFTING OTHERS UP." He encourages his players to focus both on serving, or "lifting up," each other and on serving people in need in the community.

Jesus as a Servant Leader

Throughout his time on earth, Jesus focused on the needs of others. When he saw people hungry, he fed them; when he saw people suffering from illness, he healed them; when he saw people who had sinned, he forgave them. Jesus apparently saw himself as a servant of God and the needs of others first before he saw himself as a leader.

Jesus revealed his role as a servant leader in an event that took place on his way to Jerusalem with his twelve apostles, as recorded in Mark 10:35-45. The brothers James and John asked Jesus privately if he would do a special favor for them. Jesus asked them what the favor was. James and John assumed that when Jesus arrived in Jerusalem, God would use him to depose the Roman rulers and Jewish religious leaders and set up a new kingdom with Jesus as king. James and John requested that Jesus give them special positions of power and authority in his new kingdom. Knowing that a king recognized his closest advisers by having them sit at the side of his throne, James and John asked Jesus to give them these cherished positions: one to sit on his right side and one to sit on his left when he became king. Jesus told them that they did not understand the true nature of the spiritual kingdom that he came to inaugurate.

When the other ten apostles discovered that James and John had requested key positions of honor, they were furious with these two brothers. An argument ensued and Jesus came to calm them down. Jesus explained that in the secular world, rulers demonstrated their authority over others by having others serve them. However, Jesus said that this was not the way it should be among his followers. Instead, "Whoever wishes to become great among you must be your servant, and whoever wishes to be first among you must be slave of all. For the Son of Man came not to be served but to serve, and to give his life a ransom for many" (Mark 10:43-45 NRSV).

In this teaching, Jesus makes it clear that great leaders first of all serve those they lead rather than dominate them as subordinates. Jesus not only tells his followers to become servants of others, he says that he himself came into the world "not to be served but to serve." The most effective and faithful followers of Jesus are also characterized as persons who come "not to be served but to serve" as well.

Leadership in the world is often described as a pyramid. The largest group of people, those at the base of the pyramid, are ruled by a smaller number of people on the level above them. The people on the second level are ruled by a smaller number of people on the level above them. As one moves up the pyramid, there are fewer social equals on each level and more and more people to be ruled on the levels beneath. Ultimately, the person at the top of the pyramid is seen as the great leader because this person has no equals and rules over those on all the other levels.

However, Jesus turns the leadership pyramid upside down. In an upside-down leadership pyramid, the closer one descends to the base, the more people there are above to be carried in service and love. The one at the base of an inverted pyramid is the great leader because this is the person who is committed to serving the needs of all the others on the upside-down pyramid. The one at the base of the pyramid is the servant leader to all the rest of the people in the organization.

Consequently, those who choose to become servant leaders are those who see themselves as called to serve the needs of their colleagues, customers, or clients, rather than being served by others or simply using others to achieve personal goals.

Imagine what a difference it would make in our world if political leaders, business leaders, religious leaders, university leaders, educational leaders, and leaders in all other areas of life saw themselves as first of all servants to those they are sent to serve in any particular area of life.

Other Butler Servant Leaders

Coach Stevens and the men's basketball program are not the only leaders at Butler who practice servant leadership. It is the same for the women's basketball team. Coach Couture looks almost puzzled at the thought that it would be any other way. Her players have known service throughout their young lives, she said. After all, she and her assistant coaches recruit players who bring generosity to the game, to the team, and to Butler. "They bring a passion to serve others to campus with them, and then when they are here they are beginning to see service as a way of understanding that it is bigger than you are," Couture said. "Life is about more than you and what you are doing this moment."

Born in South Bend, Indiana, Couture grew up in Greenville, South Carolina, and carved out her own playing, teaching, and coaching career in South Carolina. She was a four-year women's most valuable player at Erskine College, where she graduated in 1984. After thirteen years of coaching women's basketball and volleyball at Presbyterian College, Couture became head women's basketball coach at Butler University in 2002.

The first year she coached Butler women's basketball, the team won just six games and lost twenty-three games. She set her mind on strengthening the program by recruiting the kind of players who bring passion for the game and a willingness to grow as grateful servant leaders. With the values of the Butler Way as a foundation, Couture has steadily built an outstanding women's basketball program that has had four consecutive seasons of winning at least twenty games each season. Because of its record, the Butler women's team has been invited to play in three consecutive women's National Invitational Tournaments.

In the midst of this success in 2009, Couture received the diagnosis of stage two breast cancer. She said she feels it was the power of prayer through her family, friends, and team that enabled her to face cancer with hope and courage. The support is what allowed her to coach through the 2009–2010 season, when the Butler women finished with twenty-three victories and ten losses. Surgery, chemotherapy, and radiation over the course of an eighteen-month period led to victory over cancer. In the fall of 2010, doctors declared her cancer in remission. While the battle with breast cancer strengthened her understanding of the importance of team, with the four doctors and their staffs acting as true servant leaders through their excellent care, her family, friends, coaching colleagues, and her Butler players were also a team of loving support that surrounded her with encouragement and prayer. They were servant leaders too she said, because they led the way in lifting her spirits. She is convinced they helped her heal.

Couture has since become a key Indianapolis community leader in bringing visibility to breast cancer awareness events. She and her Butler women's team in 2011 raised more than $7,000 for breast cancer research, and she walked thirty-eight miles over a two-day span for St. Vincent Hospital Foundation's Weekend to End Breast

Cancer. During the annual walks for breast cancer, players from both the Butler women and men's teams joined her on the walk and organized rest stops for others, as well. Couture was the 2011 honorary chairwoman for the St. Vincent Women of Hope group and was also named the 2010 Woman of Distinction by Butler University as a result of her courageous and hopeful spirit in the midst of her successful cancer treatments.

Through her own experience with cancer, Couture demonstrated to her team and to the community the importance of using her leadership skills and position in the service of seeking to find a cure for breast cancer. Couture and Stevens have both become leaders in the NCAA annual Coaches vs. Cancer dinner, which raises funds to expand research and treatment for women facing breast cancer.

In all of this, Couture simply strives to model servant leadership to the team and the greater community, but she is also inspired and encouraged in her own practice of this virtue when a player brings to the team an opportunity to serve. In 2011, Butler freshman forward Haley Howard was thrilled to support breast cancer patients and decided to ask her team to help support another cancer patient, an elementary school girl from her hometown who was living with leukemia. The team planned a fund-raiser in the little girl's honor, and invited her to a special celebration during a Butler home game. "These women are learning and then going out and doing it, living it," Couture said. The players go further, volunteering to read to young children in an Indianapolis Public School near campus and visiting patients at Reilly Hospital for Children near downtown Indianapolis to encourage the kids there to remain strong in the face of their critical medical conditions.

Scott Robisch is another successful Butler servant leader. Now married with two young children, Scott is a successful sales representative for a large Indiana-based medical devices company.

The six-foot-ten forward was a freshman in 1999 for Butler's basketball team, having transferred from Oklahoma State, and played through 2002. During his Butler years the team made three trips into the NCAA tournament. Scott's father, Dave Robisch, helped the University of Kansas win the tournament in 1971 before entering the NBA. He played for the Indiana Pacers, L.A. Lakers, Denver Nuggets, and Cleveland Cavaliers. Older brother Brent played for Oklahoma State University during its NCAA tournament run in 1998. So Scott Robisch has to look no further than his family tree to understand how different it was to play for Butler compared to other, larger universities. At Butler, he discovered that the players were treated like individuals, and were expected to be adults and to follow the principles of the team on their own. Robisch described Butler as a nurturing family environment where coaches and players took a personal interest in each other and were willing to help each other succeed. Scott said that, instead of a long list of rules to be kept, the only rules at Butler were to practice the principles, be on time, attend all classes, and play hard. From day one he discovered that everyone on the team was expected to graduate, and the coaches and players were available to help students who were struggling with their classes.

Since graduating from Butler's college of business, Robisch has built a career in sales with an international medical devices manufacturer based in Indiana. The principles learned through The Butler Way have remained central to his life and to his work. He points to the practices of humility, thankfulness, and servant leadership in particular. Arrogant, hard-pushing sales representatives flame out quickly, he discovered, but those who are humble and honest with clients create relationships that, in the long run, are more productive for the customer, the sales representative, and the company. For him, gratitude is a daily practice at work, Robisch said, as well as at home, with his wife and two children. They count as blessings good health and family.

While Butler is a secular university unaffiliated with any particular religious group, Robisch found his faith life strengthened there and learned to see God as the source for blessings in his life. It was from his coaches that he learned how to put service above self and to do whatever is necessary to serve the needs of his clients and customers. A decade after leaving campus, Robisch still keeps in touch with the men on his team, and they remind each other to stay accountable to the virtues of service as they share stories of how each is active in volunteer work in his own community. "I'm blessed," Robisch said. "And I owe it all to Butler University."

Servant Leadership in Business

According to Greenleaf, the way to determine whether someone is a servant leader is to look at the people with whom that leader works. If the other people on the team are servant leaders who put the needs of others ahead of themselves, then their leader is a servant leader. In other words, judge them by their fruits. Servant leaders produce other servant leaders.

An example is Southwest Airlines, which is often held up as a model of servant leadership. Herb Kelleher, cofounder of the airline, describes the management style as an upside-down pyramid where the customers are at the top. The employees are the next level down and are employed to meet the needs of the customers. The executives are at the bottom of the upside-down pyramid and are to serve the employees so the employees can serve the customers. Each group is to serve the level above them, with the result being excellent employee and customer service. The Butler University College of Business also teaches values-based leadership principles to their students. Craig Caldwell, an assistant professor of management, maintains that the most successful business organizations build on a foundation of shared core values. He defines values as a "semi-enduring set of preferences for certain outcomes or ways of achieving them" that guide everything a company does and how it does them. Research about highly effective businesses reveals that a clear set of company values are the driving force behind high employee commitment, job satisfaction, work group effectiveness, and perceptions of the leader as charismatic. Furthermore, when there is a high correlation between the values of a company and the individual employee's personal values, there is a high degree of job engagement and job satisfaction.

Yet it is not enough for company leaders to merely post their corporate values on a wall or website. They need to practice those values consistently. Enron, the Texas-based energy futures company, was known as a place that regularly promoted corporate virtues of integrity, respect, and excellence. Yet its unethical and illegal behaviors led to its downfall. Words had little meaning in a company that failed to practice what it preached.

Successful and ethical companies thrive when they are clear about and practice their chosen values. The Butler University athletic department not only posts the values of humility, passion, unity, servanthood, thankfulness, and accountability on the walls of the locker rooms but the coach-leaders practice them. The student athletes are encouraged to incorporate these values into their lives as athletes and as future leaders in their chosen field of service.

Student Athletes Serving Others

David Woods, a reporter for the *Indianapolis Star* newspaper, wrote about Ron Nored's experience as a point guard for the Butler Bulldogs and an elementary education major at Butler University.[2] Woods pointed out that

Nored had experienced stressful moments in his four-year career on the Butler basketball team and in the thirteen NCAA tournament games in which he played. However, Nored said nothing compared to the stress he experienced as a student teacher facing thirty-two third-graders every day at the North Wayne Elementary School.

In order to complete his work and graduate as an elementary education major, Nored worked as an assistant to Mrs. Sheryl Seabrook, a seasoned third-grade teacher. Seabrook said that Nored was a role model for not only her students but for all the students in the school, and they looked up to him and listened to him. Some of the young African American students in the school may not have a positive black role model in their lives and Ron Nored helped fill that role. At Mrs. Seabrook's request, Nored worked with some of the boys with discipline problems, took the boys under his wing, mentored them, bought them books, and listened to them. Nored was particularly helpful in teaching math to the third-graders. Ron taught, coached, motivated, and cajoled students in order to help them solve their math problems. A dozen students would gather around Ron like a sideline basketball huddle as he explained math concepts.

One of the greatest needs in the United States today is more high-quality, compassionate, and competent public school teachers. Public school teachers are persons who frequently see themselves as servants to the educational needs of their students. Along with many of the other student-athletes at Butler, Ron Nored is one who has incorporated the value of servanthood in his life as an elementary school student teacher. During his four years at Butler University, he served in many other ways as well. He served as his class president, a new-student guide, a public speaker for college and community groups, a summer AAU coach for teenagers, and team co-captain in addition to being a student teacher.

On March 2, 2012, several tornadoes touched down in Indiana, Kentucky, and Alabama, killing thirty-six people and destroying towns, homes, businesses, and churches. Dozens of people were injured and families were devastated with the loss of loved ones as well as their homes and all of their possessions. St. Luke's United Methodist Church in Indianapolis, under the leadership of Senior Pastor Rob Fuquay, immediately became a collection point for urgently needed emergency supplies. When the call went out for volunteers to load and transport these supplies, Coach Stevens and his basketball team showed up and volunteered to load huge amounts of donated water, cleaning supplies, and personal care items onto the trucks, which took them to people living in temporary shelters in the tornado-ravaged areas.

A few days earlier, the Butler University team had lost a Horizon League tournament game that eliminated them from the NCAA tournament. Rather than responding to their loss with anger or despair, the Butler players immediately joined in serving the needs of those who had lost everything in the tornadoes. Instead of focusing on a lost basketball game, the Butler team focused on serving the

needs of people who had lost much. Stevens and his Butler team continue to demonstrate the value of servanthood,
whether they win or lose in basketball. They ended their
season shut out of the storied NCAA tournament. But they
also ended the season serving the needs of families and
entire communities devastated by tornados.

These athletes have had a glimpse into the world of
cancer patients. They are beginning to understand the
struggles of poor families living so close to their seemingly affluent university campus. In their careers, the athletes are modeling the characteristics of The Butler Way.
Ultimately, through serving others these athletes are learning that life is lived beyond the temporary sorrow of a lost
game or the fleeting victory of basketball success.

Coach Stevens and his team illustrate what Jesus said
about the eternal value of servanthood: "Whoever wants
to be great among you will be your servant" (Mark 10:43).

chapter five

THANKFULNESS

* *

If the only prayer you said in your whole life was "Thank You" that would be enough.
—*Meister Eckhart*

Thou hast given so much to me, give me one thing more—A Grateful Heart.
—*George Herbert*

Give thanks in all circumstances; for this is the will of God in Christ Jesus for you.
—*Paul of Tarsus (1 Thess. 5:18 NRSV)*

He fell on his face at Jesus' feet and thanked him.... Jesus replied, "Weren't ten cleansed? Where are the other nine?"
—*Jesus (Luke 17:16-17)*

According to Tracy Stevens, each year on Father's Day, Coach Brad Stevens receives several Father's Day cards from former basketball players. Why would basketball players send a Father's Day card to their former coach—someone who is not actually their father? Tracy explains that Brad frequently spends so much time listening and caring for his players—acting as a father figure—that they want to thank him in a special way.

"He is like a father, absolutely," said Ron Nored, who played for Stevens for four years. "The best fathers are the leading role models in a son's life, and he is that leading model for me, no doubt." Nored followed Stevens into coaching, landing a high school coaching position in suburban Indianapolis even before graduating with his degree in elementary education. His own father died when Ron was just thirteen, so this young coach knows what it means to need that presence in one's life. He said, "All of my life I will be thankful for what Coach Stevens means to me."

On one occasion, a Butler basketball player was injured and had to have emergency surgery at a hospital. Stevens, who as head coach could have dispatched an assistant or a team trainer, spent a whole night in the hospital waiting room to see how the surgery came out and to offer support and encouragement to that injured player. This young man is one of the players who still regularly expresses thankfulness to his former coach for his compassionate care.

As a regular practice, Coach Stevens puts an encouraging quotation on each player's locker before a practice or a game. This is one of the ways that Coach Stevens expresses his gratitude to each of his players and becomes a father-like encourager for them as basketball players and as persons.

Here are some of his favorites:

Be the change you want to see.

You grow through what you go through.

No excuses, no explanations.

Make the main thing, the main thing.

There is a difference between success and significance.

When Coach Stevens places thoughtful and encouraging quotations on the players' lockers, it reminds them that he is thinking about them all the time and how he wants to encourage their personal growth. Consequently, it is not surprising that players frequently express gratitude to their coach, because he cares for them and their growth—like a good father cares for his children.

The fifth value promoted in Butler basketball is simply expressed as thankfulness. It means to be full of thanks in the midst of every circumstance. One can be thankful in every circumstance because there is something one can learn from every circumstance one faces in life. The Butler coaches teach that even when they lose a game and get discouraged, they remember there is always something they can learn from that losing experience to improve their performance in the next game. Butler summarizes this value simply as, "Learn from every circumstance."

The truth is that everyone will go through discouraging times in life. We may lose a loved one or a job or our health or a marriage or a championship game. In times like these it is easy to become discouraged, disappointed, and depressed. When things go wrong in our lives, it is easy to become negative and cynical and want to give up. In the face of disappointment in life, a person can choose two responses: to become bitter or to become better. The world is full of bitter and cynical people for whom life has not turned out the way they wanted. Yet there are others who have experienced exactly the same challenges in life but have used them as opportunities for growth and learning. Ultimately, we can be thankful even for the difficulties we face, because they help us grow to become deeper, wiser, and more compassionate persons. We always have a choice whether challenges in life will make us bitter or make us better.

This is what Paul meant when he told the people in Thessalonica to "give thanks in all circumstances."

Paul came to Thessalonica, the capital of Macedonia, on his second missionary journey. He preached in the local synagogue the good news of God's unconditional love that comes to us in Jesus Christ. Paul called Christ followers to "be at peace among yourselves....Rejoice always [and] pray without ceasing" (1 Thess. 5:13, 16-17 NRSV). Many people became followers of Jesus, but many others were aroused to oppose this new teaching about a God who raised Jesus from death to life. Consequently, Paul's opponents drove him out of Thessalonica, then followed him to Beroea (Berea), where they opposed him and again drove him out of town. Paul went through beatings, imprisonments, shipwreck, and starvation, but he continued to share the good news of Jesus Christ in spite of all these sufferings.

In spite of the hardships he faced, Paul lived a life of continual thanksgiving. He began his first letter to the Thessalonians by expressing his thanksgiving to God: "We always give thanks to God for all of you and mention you in our prayers, constantly remembering before our God and Father your work of faith and labor of love and steadfastness of hope in our Lord Jesus Christ" (1 Thess. 1:2 NRSV).

Paul was a man who had experienced great sufferings in his life and yet he could write, "give thanks in all circumstances" (1 Thess. 5:17 NRSV). Paul did not say, "Give thanks FOR all circumstances." He was not asking followers to be thankful for the suffering and deaths they experienced. Rather, he said that in the midst of every circumstance, there is always something for which to be thankful. We are not thankful that a loved one died or that a friend contracted a chronic or deadly disease. But in the midst of those difficulties we discover that for which we can be thankful.

In the midst of the loss of a loved one, we can be thankful for the gifts of life they shared with us while they were in this world. We can be thankful for their gift of eternal life and the loving support of family and friends whose love lifts us up and keeps us going. In the midst of illness we can be thankful for the loving support of the medical profession and the prayers for healing of people who care for us. And, in the midst of the loss of an NCAA championship game, a basketball team can be thankful for the opportunity to play in a championship game with team members who care about each other, a coaching staff committed to their growth, and the loving support of fans and friends all around the world.

Thankfulness means to give thanks in all circumstances because we can learn and grow from every circumstance we face in life.

We may find it easy to express what is sometimes called conditional gratitude. When things are going well in our families, our business, and our personal relationships, it is much easier to express gratitude and thanksgiving to God for all the blessings in our lives. When our life conditions are pleasant, our health is good, and we have an abundance of positive blessings, we find it easier to give thanks.

However, a deeper level of gratitude is called unconditional gratitude. Unconditional gratitude occurs regardless of the conditions in our lives at any given moment. Unconditional gratitude means to give thanks to God even in times of difficulty and suffering, as Paul did. When Paul tells us to "give thanks in all circumstances" he encourages us to move from conditional gratitude that expresses thankfulness when things are going well to unconditional gratitude, in which we express thankfulness to God regardless of whether good or bad things are happening in our lives at any given moment.

Thankfulness may be the most difficult of values to live inside the world of high-stakes college athletics. Dick Bennett, a legendary men's college coach at the University of Wisconsin and Washington State University, said he believes it to be so. And Bennett should know. During the 1990s he created a simple one-page document that inspired The Butler Way. At the time he was coaching the men at Wisconsin-Madison, leading a program that would go to the NCAA Division I Final Four in Indianapolis. Thankfulness was easy during that tournament run, Bennett recalls. But during the 1985–1986 season at University of Wisconsin–Green Bay, when the team was 5 and 26, gratitude was hard to muster. "When you come off of a win, it is easy to say I am grateful for how well we played or for having these good kids. But being always joyful, always grateful? When we lose, when we get a bad whistle? Yes. We are to be thankful in all things. *All* is the operative word here because it includes those difficult times. That is where the wisdom is," he said.

For Bennett, it is the wisdom of faith—of his own Christian faith—that has been strengthened by the discipline of gratitude in the darkest times.

Gratefulness Leads to Great Fullness

When we live a life of gratefulness in the midst of all circumstances of life, we experience great fullness in our lives.

Dr. Robert Emmons is a psychology professor at the

University of California in Davis, California. Dr. Emmons's foremost interest lies in the psychology of gratitude and the psychology of personal goals. Dr. Emmons conducted a study in which he asked one group of student volunteers to keep a gratitude journal, where they would write down everything they were grateful for each day for two months. He asked a second group of student volunteers to keep a negative journal in which they would write down all the negative events that occurred in their lives each day for two months.

Dr. Emmons interviewed all of the students in the experiment and discovered that those who kept gratitude journals felt better about their lives, exercised more, reported fewer physical symptoms, and were more optimistic about the week ahead. The group recording their daily negative events did not show any positive results in these areas of life.

When it came to setting personal goals, the gratitude journal group made great progress toward health goals, academic goals, and interpersonal goals, while the other group failed to make any progress toward the goals they had previously set for themselves.

Emmons also conducted another study with young adults that involved daily gratitude self-guided exercises. These young adults reported higher levels of positive states of alertness, enthusiasm, determination, attentiveness, and energy compared to those who focused on the hassles and difficulties of their daily lives. Those who participated in the daily gratitude exercises were also more likely to help someone with a personal problem or offer emotional support to another person than those in the negative group.

Furthermore, in a sample of adults with neuromuscular disease, Emmons conducted a twenty-one-day gratitude intervention that resulted in greater amounts of high-energy, positive moods, a greater sense of feeling connected to others, more optimistic ratings of one's life, and better sleep duration and sleep quality compared to a control group.[1]

The results of these studies indicate that when one lives a life of gratefulness, one has greater fullness in life. People who learn to express their gratitude and count their blessings in life tend to have better health and happiness and more compassion for those in need than those who focus on the negative aspects of their lives. On the whole, persons who live lives with an attitude of gratitude live fuller and happier lives than those who focus their attention on their problems and the negative things that happen in their lives.

A Christian hymn has it this way: "Count your many blessings, name them one by one; count your many blessings, see what God has done."[2] When people focus on counting their blessings, they discover that they have more blessings than they were aware of and consequently feel grateful for those blessings.

The effect of thankfulness is more than mere self-help pop psychology. What we count we tend to increase. When we count our blessings, it seems as though we ultimately have more blessings to count. When we count our woes and problems, we seem to have more woes and problems to count. Everyone knows people who continually recount all the problems they have experienced in life, and each time you encounter them they seem to have new and more problems to share. Some people seem to be on the constant lookout for the negative aspects of life to complain about, which decreases their feelings of joy and fulfillment in life.

Gratefulness leads to greater fullness in life, and negativity leads to less fullness in life.

Thankful Basketball Players

Gordon Hayward is a former Butler player who has gone on to play in the NBA with the Utah Jazz. Hayward and his family continually thank God for their faith and trust in God, for his surprising growth as a basketball player, his academic abilities, and for the opportunities to be a positive, values-based witness in the National Basketball Association.

Gordon played both basketball and tennis at the Brownsburg High School in Indiana, and thought that tennis would be the sport he would excel in. At five foot eleven, his height seemed to limit how good he could be as a basketball player. Both of his parents are of average height, so it wasn't expected for him to be much taller than they are. Because of this, his father encouraged him to develop his ball handling and long-range shooting skills as a guard so that with those skills he might make the high school basketball team. Unexpectedly, Hayward experienced a growth spurt in high school and shot up to six foot four as a sophomore and six foot eight as a senior. He became the star player on the Brownsburg basketball team and was named to the All-State team in 2008. In the 2008 Class 4A State Championship game, Gordon hit the game-winning layup at the buzzer to defeat Marion High School, 40-39.

Pat Forde, an ESPN.com columnist, said that Gordon Hayward was a guy who learned to play like a guard, but who has the size of a power forward, largely because of his father's wrong guess about his future growth potential. Gordon Hayward went to Butler University to play under Coach Brad Stevens while his twin sister, Heather, attended Butler to play tennis. Gordon made an instant impact on Butler basketball as a freshman in 2008–2009. Butler had lost four starting players from the year before and was projected to finish fifth in the Horizon League. However, the Bulldogs went 26-5 and won the Horizon League. Hayward averaged 13.1 points per game and 6.5 rebounds and was named the Horizon League Newcomer of the Year and selected for the All-Conference team.

As a sophomore in 2009–2010, Gordon Hayward was the only player to finish in the Horizon League's top five in both scoring and rebounding. He was named the Horizon League's Player of the Year and to the ESPN's Academic All-American team. In the 2010 NCAA tournament, Gordon Hayward was named the Most Valuable Player of the

West Region as he led Butler to the national championship game. In the championship game against Duke University, which would have given Butler their very first NCAA championship, he missed the game-winning half-court shot by an inch.

After just two years on the Butler team, Hayward was recruited to play professional basketball by NBA scouts. It was a tough decision for Hayward and his family; however, they decided to put it in the hands of God. They offered prayers thanking God for Hayward's amazing basketball talent and for his sincerity of faith. They prayed that God would give them guidance on this life-changing decision.

After several talks with Coach Stevens, who supported whatever decision they made, and with NBA scouts, they finally decided to allow Hayward to leave college as a sophomore to enter the NBA draft.

Drafted by the Utah Jazz, Hayward had an impressive first year. When the Utah Jazz played the Los Angeles Lakers, Hayward defended Kobe Bryant from the Lakers, causing Bryant to commit seven turnovers and make just six of eighteen shots. Hayward finished the game with twenty-two points and six rebounds, making several clutch plays in the final minutes of a Utah 86-85 victory over Los Angeles.

Avery Jukes is another former Butler basketball player who expresses his gratitude for his blessings through his service to others. Jukes was an All-State forward at South

Gwinnett High School in Snellville, Georgia, and as a high school sophomore helped lead his team to thirty wins and three losses and a Georgia state championship. At six foot eight, Jukes was named a Nike All-American as a senior and was on the All-Conference team. After one year at the University of Alabama, he transferred to Butler University, where he played for the Butler Bulldogs for three years and helped the team win victories in three NCAA tournaments. He graduated from Butler with a bachelor of arts degree in mechanical engineering and mathematics in 2010.

While at Butler, Jukes travelled to Uganda with Ambassadors for Children to help build a school for children with few opportunities for an education. Jukes spent ten days working with a team from the United States, clearing land and building a foundation for a school building. It changed his perspective on life. He spent much of his time with the children and discovered how difficult and challenging their lives were. In the midst of this great poverty, he realized how blessed he was and made a decision to express his gratitude for his blessings by raising funds to help support the children he had met in Uganda.

After returning to the United States, Jukes started the Jukes Foundation for Kids to provide educational opportunities for children in Uganda. He has sponsored fundraising activities at Butler University and the Indianapolis community to raise funds for educational scholarships for children who otherwise would not be able to pay the modest tuition to attend schools in Uganda. The Jukes Foundation has also helped build a primary school with seven classrooms and a library. Every year Jukes visits Uganda to provide hands-on humanitarian service to children in need.

Avery Jukes realized that he has been exceedingly blessed compared to the students he met in Uganda and he expressed his gratitude for his blessings by giving back and serving some of the educational needs of children in Uganda. Coach Stevens has praised Avery Jukes for upholding the Butler values of thankfulness and servanthood through his compassionate service to others and for the way he makes a positive difference in the lives of children in need.

Blessed but Not Grateful

Some people recognize that they are blessed and find ways to express gratitude, while others receive the same blessings but take them for granted and fail to express gratitude for the blessings they have received in their lives.

The seventeenth chapter of Luke's Gospel tells such a story. Jesus was on his way from Galilee in the north to Jerusalem in the south when he passed through the region of Samaria. On the outskirts of one of the villages there was a group of ten lepers. In the time of Jesus, lepers had to live outside a village and keep a stone's throw away from other people so they did not infect them with the disease. As Jesus neared the village, the ten lepers came as close as they could and cried out, "Jesus, Master, have mercy on us!"

Jesus stopped and looked at these excluded lepers with compassion. Then he told them to go into the village and allow the priest to examine them to verify that they were healed and could return to live with their families in the village. Nine of the healed lepers were so excited to be free of disease that they ran to the priest for examination. However, one of the healed lepers, when he realized that he had been healed, was so filled with gratitude that he turned around and ran back to Jesus. He fell at the feet of Jesus, loudly praising and thanking God for his healing. Then Jesus asked, "Were not ten made clean? But the other nine, where are they? Was none of them found to return and give praise to God except this foreigner?" (Luke 17:17-18 NRSV).

The other nine received the blessing of healing but failed to thank God for the blessing.

In a similar way, many of us are glad to receive the blessings of life, love, family, home, country, and the natural world from the hand of God. However, like the nine lepers, we often receive God's blessings, take them for granted, and fail to kneel before God to express our gratitude.

Leaders who choose to lead like Butler will be persons who recognize all the gifts they have already received from God and will not only give thanks for their many blessings but also will follow the example of Paul and "give thanks in all circumstances."

ACCOUNTABILITY

You must take personal responsibility. You cannot change the circum-
stances, the seasons or the wind, but you can change yourself.
—Jim Rohn

Be the change you want to see in the world.
—Mahatma Gandhi

When a man points a finger at someone else, he should remember that
four of his fingers are pointing at himself.
—Louis Nizer, lawyer and author

"Why do you see the speck in your neighbor's eye, but do not notice the
log in your own eye?"
—Jesus (Matt. 7:3 NRSV)

Since the beginning of the 2002–2003 basketball season, Coach Brad Stevens requires all of his new players to
read the book *The Question Behind the Question: Prac-*
ticing Personal Accountability at Work and Life by John
G. Miller. Before the first practice, each player personally speaks with the coach and submits a one-page paper
on what he gained from the book. Personal accountability

has become so important to the Butler team that Coach Stevens added accountability to the other five principles originally articulated by Barry Collier.

When we ask questions that begin with "Why" "Who," or "When" and contain a "they," "them," "we," or "you," we invariably fall into blaming, complaining, and procrastinating. These nonproductive questions lead to division and ineffectiveness. Nonproductive questions asked by management are questions like, "Who dropped the ball on this project?" or "When are they going to catch the vision?" Questions like "How can I be a better leader?" or "How can I communicate the vision better?" have a much better chance of improving the climate for everyone. A worker's nonproductive question might be "When are we going to get a better boss?" or "Why don't they listen to us?" Better to ask, "How can I be a better leader where I am?" or "How can I listen and communicate better?" But no matter what your job or position in the workplace, personal accountability means asking yourself what you can do, rather than blaming someone else or complaining about the actions of *that other person*.

Whenever Coach Stevens hears a player blame another player for a mistake or complain about a situation, he gets their attention and simply says "QBQ." It is the coach's way of reminding players to simply ask themselves, "What can I do to make this situation better?" rather than complaining or blaming someone else for the problems at hand.

Personal accountability questions enable us to avoid blaming and complaining and focus our attention on an action that we can perform that will improve the situation. The truth is we cannot change other people; we can only change ourselves. When we make the positive changes we can make the situation will improve and move in a positive direction for everyone.

The emphasis on personal accountability has paid off for Coach Stevens and the Butler program. Sports reporters have noted that Butler University basketball players are rarely found blaming other players for a loss, blaming the coaching staff, or complaining about the other team. They quickly accept whatever the problems are and move forward with what each of them can do personally to improve the situation, asking, "What can I do to make it better?"

Personal Accountability at Butler

Midway through the 2010–2011 schedule, Butler lost four out of five games in a row, dropping their conference record to 6-5. With only seven games remaining in the season, starting with a trip to the home of the top-ranked Cleveland State Vikings, sportswriters predicted that Butler would not repeat the success they'd had in the previous NCAA championship game. Before Butler took the court against Cleveland State, star player Shelvin Mack asked the coach for permission to speak to his fellow teammates. Mack gave his teammates a simple message: we all need to do better, and it starts with me. He explained that he knew he was not playing to his highest potential and committed himself to giving more of himself to the team. He took personal responsibility for improving his own game for the sake of the team.

To the surprise of everyone, Butler beat Cleveland State, 73-61. They closed the season on a seven-game winning streak, tying the Vikings for first place in the conference. They won both conference tournament games, five straight NCAA tournament games, and once again played in the NCAA championship game. Coach Stevens says that Shelvin Mack's statement of personal accountability, encouraging all the players to improve themselves, turned their season around.

The next season, 2011–2012, brought new trials. While expectations grew higher and the schedule grew tougher, the team lost several talented and seasoned players. With a young lineup, they began the year with several losses, many to teams they had beaten in the past. It would have been easy for coaches and players to start blaming each other for their poor performance. However, even after losses, players and coaches refused to blame anyone else. They simply talked about what they personally needed to do to help turn the season around and start winning games again.

In one loss, senior Ron Nored scored a career-high seventeen points, leading his team with great energy and enthusiasm. It may have been tempting for him to blame other players for failing to score or defend or rebound as well as they should have. He could have felt that he did his part in scoring but that the other team members were not playing as well as they should have been and they were the reason for the loss. However, Ron Nored did not respond in any of these negative ways. When he was interviewed by a reporter, he said, "It's about finishing, which honestly I haven't done very well this year up to this point." Nored never said a word about other players' shortcomings. He only focused on the one thing he could control: how he needed to improve his own performance at the end of games for the sake of the whole team.

About their poor win-loss record at the beginning of the 2011–2012 season, Coach Stevens said, "If you focus too much on what your record is, you're not going to get better. If you've got something that's not going your way, work through it. Do it harder. Do it better. Pay more attention to it." The coach never criticizes any player. He just encourages each individual to focus on improving themselves in the ways they can and to know that the team will thrive as a result.

In spite of their struggles in 2011–2012, the young team won many games against favored teams. When players are taught not to blame or complain but simply to focus on personal improvement, the whole team does better.

Khyle Marshall has been a very good player at Butler. The six-foot-six sophomore power forward from Davie, Florida, had a 2011 NCAA Tournament-best twenty-three offensive rebounds in six games. In one game at the beginning of the 2011–2012 year, he scored twenty-one points and made sixteen rebounds. However, as the season went on, he found himself playing fewer and fewer minutes as two freshmen players spent more time on the court in his power forward spot. When a reporter asked Marshall about playing fewer minutes, Marshall responded, "I just need to keep a steady head, keep my head straight, and look to the future. I can't look back on previous games. I know my team will need me down the road, so I just need to be ready to do whatever I can."

The reporter was obviously baiting Marshall to see if he would criticize the coach or the new freshmen players with whom he was sharing his minutes on the court. However, Marshall didn't take the bait and simply talked about how he had to continue to focus on improving his own game. The reporter asked a why question: "Why aren't you getting more minutes of playing time this year?" Marshall responded by answering a what question: "What can I do to improve my game so I can make a better contribution to my team in the future?"

When basketball players, political leaders, business leaders, religious leaders, educators, family members, or anyone else refuse to blame or complain in any situation, positive results follow. People in every area of life blame and complain, seemingly about almost everything, which creates a negative, pessimistic cloud over the whole society. This blaming, finger-pointing game prevents us from taking positive actions we each could take. Often, you can't change circumstances, the season, the wind, or the day of the week, but you can change yourself. Or, as Mahatma Gandhi said when he called people to personal responsibility: "Be the change you want to see in the world."

Jesus and Judging Others

In the Sermon on the Mount, Jesus speaks about judging others with these words:

> "Don't judge, so that you won't be judged. You'll receive the same judgment you give. Whatever you deal out will be dealt out to you. Why do you see the splinter that's in your brother's or sister's eye, but don't notice the log in your own eye? How can you say to your brother or sister, 'Let me take the splinter out of your eye,' when there's a log in your eye? You deceive yourself! First take the log out of your eye, and then you'll see clearly to take the splinter out of your brother's or sister's eye." (Matt. 7:1-5)

Sadly, non-Christians often describe Christians as judgmental toward everyone who is not a follower of Jesus. Christians are often experienced as self-righteous and condemning, even toward other Christians with whom they disagree. However, Jesus encouraged his followers not to judge others harshly: "For with the judgment you make you will be judged" (Matt. 7:2 NRSV). In other words, if we judge and condemn others harshly, then we too will be judged and condemned harshly for the shortcomings in our lives. Conversely, if we are compassionate and forgiving in our attitudes toward others and their shortcomings, then God will be compassionate and forgiving toward us as well.

When Jesus talks about seeing the splinter in your neighbor's eye, he is talking about our human tendency to see clearly the faults in others and focus our attention on their shortcomings rather than recognizing our own shortcomings and seeking to improve ourselves. Jesus contrasts the small "splinter" in our neighbor's eye with the huge "log" in our own eye. We frequently fail to see our own shortcomings, even though they may be large and obvious to others. It is as if we focus our attention on the shortcomings of others so that we can avoid dealing with our own failures.

The Butler principle of accountability does not make judgments on other people but rather emphasizes personal accountability and holding ourselves responsible to do whatever we can to improve every situation in which we find ourselves.

Jesus taught and practiced forgiving others rather than judging or condemning them. In the Lord's Prayer, Jesus said, "Forgive us for the ways we have wronged you, / just as we also forgive those who have wronged us" (Matt. 6:12). At the end of the Lord's Prayer he again emphasized the importance of forgiveness when he said, "If you forgive others their sins, your heavenly Father will also forgive you. But if you don't forgive others, neither will your Father forgive your sins" (Matt. 6:14). Jesus also practiced forgiveness rather than condemnation when some Pharisees brought a woman caught in an adulterous act to him.

Early in the morning he returned to the temple. All the people gathered around him, and he sat down and taught them. The legal experts and Pharisees brought a woman caught in adultery. Placing her in the center of the group, they said to Jesus, "Teacher, this woman was caught in the act of committing adultery. In the Law, Moses commanded us to stone women like this. What do you say?" They said this to test him, because they wanted a reason to bring an accusation against him. Jesus bent down and wrote on the ground with his finger. They continued to question him, so he stood up and replied, "Whoever hasn't sinned should throw the first stone." Bending down again, he wrote on the ground. Those who heard him went away, one by one, beginning with the elders. Finally, only Jesus and the woman were left in the middle of the crowd. Jesus stood up and said to her, "Woman, where are they? Is there no one to condemn you?" She said, "No one, sir." Jesus said, "Neither do I condemn you. Go, and from now on, don't sin anymore." (John 8:2-11)

The scribes and Pharisees remind Jesus that the Law of Moses says that she should be stoned to death. Actually, there are two places in the Hebrew Scriptures where Jewish leaders are commanded to stone to death both the man and the woman who commit adultery (Lev. 20:10 and Deut. 22:22-24). Interestingly, and in a commentary on the social dynamics of the ethics of the Law in Jesus' time, the scribes and the Pharisees only bring the woman to be stoned to death. They released the man also involved in the adulterous act rather than bringing him to Jesus for judgment as well.

Jesus bent down and wrote something on the ground with his finger. Many believe that Jesus may have written down the sins of her accusers. He may have written something like "self-righteous, judgmental, arrogant, egotistical." When Jesus finished writing whatever he wrote, he looked at her adversaries and said, "Let anyone among you who is without sin be the first to throw a stone at her."

When her accusers heard his words and perhaps saw their sins written plainly on the ground in front of them, they went away and left Jesus and the woman alone. The story concluded when Jesus said to the woman: "Neither do I condemn you. Go your way, and from now on do not sin again."

Jesus practiced forgiveness rather than judgment and condemnation for someone who had sinned and fallen short of the mark of God's desire for her life.

Later, when Jesus was crucified, those who crucified him stood at the foot of the cross gloating over their victory. One of the final actions of Jesus before he died was to ask God to forgive those who conspired to kill him. Jesus prayed: "Father, forgive them, for they don't know what they're doing" (Luke 23:34).

Louis Nizer, noted lawyer and author of *My Life in Court* (1961), wrote, "When a man points a finger at someone else, he should remember that four of his fingers are pointing at himself." Coach Stevens often uses the "four fingers pointing at himself" illustration with his team to remind them not to point to the mistakes of other teammates but to focus on themselves and how they can personally improve as basketball players and as persons.

After Butler lost the 2010 NCAA Championship game to Duke University, Coach Stevens was interviewed on the David Letterman show. Letterman tried to bait Stevens by telling him that Michigan State coach Tom Izzo had predicted that Duke would beat Butler by ten to fifteen points or more. Letterman then asked: "Why would Izzo say something stupid like that?"

Coach Sevens responded by saying, "He knows a lot more about basketball than I do. We were just privileged to be on the court with great teams like Michigan State and Duke."

Letterman: "You're not going to take my bait, are you?"

Stevens: "I'm too young to take your bait!"[2]

Stevens refused to criticize another coach for his negative assessment of Butler's chances against Duke but simply acknowledged that he felt honored to be on the court with such great teams as Michigan State and Duke. Stevens demonstrated both a refusal to criticize anyone else and a level of humility by saying that his team was honored to be on the court with teams from traditionally great basketball programs.

Miller concludes *The Question Behind the Question* with an amazing story about the benefits of personally doing whatever it takes to serve your customer or client.

Judy was a cashier at a Home Depot store. A young man came through her line in a hurry. He laid down a few items worth two dollars and eighty-nine cents and gave Judy a $100 bill.

Judy asked, "Do you have anything smaller?"

The young man answered, "No, I'm sorry. I don't."

Judy had only $40 in change in her drawer, so she would normally have to put the $100 bill in a pneumatic tube and send it up to the office to make the proper change. But Judy realized that it would take time, the young man was in a hurry, and there were other customers waiting in line.

Judy did something highly unusual. She handed the young man his $100 bill back, reached down for her purse, took out $2.89, and put it in the drawer. Then she gave the young man his receipt, smiled at him, and said: "Thanks for shopping at Home Depot." The young man was shocked by what she had done. He thanked her profusely for personally paying his bill and left the store amazed at what had just happened.

The next day the young man showed up in Judy's check-out line again, but this time he was with his father, who owned a very large construction company. The father said to Judy, "I want you to know that because of what you did to serve my son the other day, we've decided to start getting all of our building supplies from Home Depot."

Judy could have been upset because someone gave her such a large bill for such a small purchase. She could have just made him and all the other customers wait while she got change from the office. But rather than complaining or blaming, Judy asked herself, "What can I do to make this situation better?" Her answer was to simply pay the small bill herself so the young man and all the other customers in line would receive quicker service. The end result of a cashier doing what she could to make the situation better was that her company received a large contract for building supplies.

Coach Stevens's Signs on Accountability

Coach Stevens has great admiration for former Indianapolis Colts coach Tony Dungy, who made famous the phrase "No Excuses, No Explanations." After a losing game, sports reporters frequently interview the losing coach for an explanation about why they lost the game. When the Colts lost a game, Coach Dungy never made excuses for his team, nor did he explain the loss by blaming anyone else. Dungy would frequently compliment the other team on their excellent offense or defense and talk about what he needed to do with his team to improve their weaknesses before the next game. Coach Dungy saw every lost game simply as an opportunity for growth, and focused on what he and his coaching staff needed to do to improve their team's performance the next week. Coach Dungy practiced personal accountability and focused on what he could do to improve his team rather than complaining about the situation or blaming someone else for the loss.

Drew Streicher was a six-foot-seven guard/forward

for the Butler Bulldogs from 2005 to 2008, when he graduated as an Academic All-American and outstanding player. On the wall in the men's locker room Coach Stevens has placed this quotation from Streicher:

> It's more of a culture than a concept. It begins with personal accountability and putting your teammates above yourself. Then it's playing the game with passion, giving your all, all the time, making the extra pass, getting the extra rebound. Off the courts, it's conducting yourself in a way that represents Butler the best you can.

"It begins with personal accountability and putting your teammates above yourself" would be a good way to summarize the Butler way and the Butler principles.

Coach Stevens has also placed a plaque in the Butler locker room listing all of the Butler players who have been Academic All-Americans. The players listed on that plaque are: J. Graves, 2007, 2008; Drew Streicher, 2008; Matt Howard, 2009, 2010; and Gordon Hayward, 2010. Coach Stevens honors the Academic All-Americans who have played Butler basketball because he recognizes the importance of getting a good education at Butler as well as being a good athlete.

Coach Stevens constantly reminds his players to attend every class every day, even when the professor may not require class attendance, and to study hard to the best of their ability. When the team is on the road, the student athletes are expected to take their homework with them because they can't use basketball as an excuse for failing to get their class work in on time. If a student is having trouble with a class, the coach will provide a tutor for him and check with him regularly to see how he is doing.

When student athletes are not doing well in class, Coach Stevens will say "no excuses, no explanations" as a way to motivate them not to make excuses or blame a particular situation for their academic shortcomings. They are simply expected to be personally accountable for getting their academic work done and graduating from college and being successful in their chosen field.

Personal accountability is of high value both on the court and in the classroom at Butler. Each player signs a statement of accountability each year, and it's placed on the wall in the player's locker room for all to see. The statement, originally written by Coach Todd Lickliter, says:

> We acknowledge the privilege and responsibility inherent with being a Bulldog and will immerse ourselves in The Butler Way thus enhancing the Butler experience for the entire Butler community.

Their signatures are the way they hold themselves personally accountable to uphold the Butler principles of leadership: Humility, Passion, Unity, Servanthood, Thankfulness, and Accountability.

EPILOGUE

For a long time a simple photograph was on the official team web page. It was similar to the image on the cover of this book, and it spoke volumes—a thousand words, as the saying goes—about a central idea: team. It showed fifteen young men at center court, huddled, heads down, almost in a kind of reverence or prayer. Their backs were to the camera and the world. Numbers on their blue jerseys were covered by a common uniform. The players' individual identities were blurred. There is only team. In the end, it is about team. After all, when many of us watch a college basketball game, we cheer not for a person but for a team—a uniform and logo that represents a special place in our hearts. Perhaps it is the school where we learned and came of age as students, years before. Or it's the team from a school in which we longed to have been a part.

Of course, all teams share common goals, to come together, outscore the opponent, and defend home. The team at Butler succeeds when the virtues of The Butler Way come together, when there is an integration of humility, passion, unity, servanthood, thankfulness, and accountability.

The team in that photo soared to unimagined success in back-to-back appearances in the NCAA Final Four, and then in spring 2012 didn't even make it into that famed and storied tournament. Some sports journalists described the Cinderella story as over, the glass slipper cracked. But if the fairy tale captured the imagination of a nation of college basketball fanatics and even inspired new fans, it is precisely the wonder of it all that allows a less-than-perfect team to continue to teach.

Each of us is less than perfect. As business leaders, teachers, community activists, parents, spouses, pastors, and congregants, we strive to be our best. Many times, we fall short. We know how hard it is, so we keep looking for insight and inspiration. We know that perhaps most of all it is when we do not soar that our deepest commitments keep us upright. When we keep faith in the hardest of times, we experience more fully the goodness of it all.

So the 2011–2012 Butler team, ending its season at 22-15, has much to teach the team coming up behind it. It was a young team. Since well before the start of the season, Coach Stevens was calmly, clearly stating this truth. Six of the fifteen players were freshmen. Without apology or fear, Stevens was telling fans, sports writers, administrators, anyone with an expectation of a third straight NCAA tournament run, that this team was dominated by freshmen. Three seniors were back, and they would be stellar leaders. But Shelvin Mack, who as a sophomore and junior was part of those Cinderella teams of 2010 and 2011, had moved to the NBA. So had Gordon Haywood, another young man who would likely have been in his seasoned senior year if he had not left for the NBA in 2010, after just two years at Butler.

"We have young guys, and we have a lot to do together to become the team I know we can become," Stevens said before the season opened. This was never intended to be an excuse or a reason to expect anything less than excellence. But the reality is that new players need to be trained in The Butler Way. They may bring passion and even a basic understanding of service and unity. But integrating these virtues and learning about what humility, servanthood, thankfulness, gratitude, and accountability mean on the court takes time—lots of practice, teaching, and patience, balanced with focus. Reflecting on this season in the calm that comes after, Stevens spoke about basketball skills and then about a greater vision for his students. "I think we were lacking in the technical. We need to score. We need to be better at ball handling, shooting, and defense. It is that clear," Stevens said. "But what I also saw was a team that stayed together. I saw our older guys truly encourage the freshmen, truly teach them how to stay together. I could not have asked for a better expression of that than what I saw in Ron."

Ronald Nored ended his college basketball career as one of those leaders. After the season closed, the education major from Mississippi announced that following graduation from Butler he would become the boys' basketball coach at Brownsburg High School in the western suburbs of Indianapolis. His degree from the Butler

College of Education, combined with his years on the court with Coach Stevens, provides a solid foundation for his calling to teach and lead.

Just like his mentor, Coach Stevens, Nored did not mince words about a disappointing season. Like Stevens, he is passionate about winning. The Bulldogs lost games they needed to win, he said. They didn't compete at the level they had hoped for. And this was the last shot for Nored, the player who had been to the Final Four twice. Yes, there was disappointment and sadness. But there was clarity about what it means to lead, and about faith. "The thing that kept me going were my teammates. I have to leave here, but they have to stay, they have to carry on the next year. They need to be left with positive energy and deeper understanding about the way things are done here. That is what was handed down to me, and I needed to push myself so I could help hand it down to them."

In 2010, Butler University experienced a kind of magic when its Bulldogs surprised everybody with a run to the pinnacle of college athletic competition. Their un-imagined visit to the Final Four, being played in their hometown, inspired a deeper exploration about how it was possible for a small school to compete at such a great level. Everyone learned about the ingredients known as The Butler Way. They really add up to something simple, if not simplistic. "Just doing the right thing, every day," is how Butler's women's coach, Beth Couture, explains it. "Every day" means when the team wins and when it doesn't.

In the afterglow of the Bulldogs' 2010 season, Susan Neville, an Indiana writer and Butler professor of English, wrote a book called *Butler's Big Dance: The Team, The Tournament, and Basketball Fever* (Indiana University Press, 2010). It is not really a basketball book, but rather a kind of meditation on a place that brings students like Ron Nored into its classrooms. It is about a place that allows a coach like Brad Stevens to teach more than a game.

The final pages of her meditation are not about the tournament at all. Instead, they are filled with word pictures from the summer youth basketball camp Coach Stevens and his wife produce each June in Hinkle Fieldhouse. It's the same camp experience they created before the Final Four runs. The same one they shared after it. After stellar seasons and seasons that leave behind longing, a new group of young collegiate players help Stevens staff the drills and clinics for third- and fourth-graders and middle-schoolers too. There is, after all, a team to build, Stevens said.

"Every day we get a shot at building it."

NOTES

Introduction

1. *Indianapolis Star*, February 18, 2012, sec. C5.

2. Ibid.

3. Pat Williams, with David Wimbish, *How to Be Like Coach Wooden: Life Lessons from Basketball's Greatest Leader* (Deerfield Beach, FL: HCI, 2006), 5, 29.

4. Tony Dungy, with Nathan Whitaker, *Quiet Strength: The Principles, Practices, and Priorities of a Winning Life* (Carol Stream, IL: Tyndale House, 2007), xv.

5. Tony Dungy with Jim Caldwell and Nathan Whitaker, *The Mentor Leader: Secrets to Building People and Teams That Win Consistently* (Carol Stream, IL: Tyndale House: 2010).

1. Humility

1. James O'Toole, *Leading Change: The Argument for Values-Based Leadership* (New York: Ballantine, 1996), 10–11.

2. Tony Dungy and Nathan Whitaker, *Uncommon: Finding Your Path to Significance* (Carol Stream, IL: Tyndale, 2011), 19.

2. Passion

1. Dan Wetzel, http://rivals.yahoo.com/ncaa/basketball/news?slug=dw-wetzel_final_four_butler_goes_down_its_way_040511 Yahoo!, 4/5/11.

2. Rudyard Kipling, "If." Originally published in "Brother Square Toes," in *Rewards and Fairies*, 1910.

3. Marianne Williamson, *A Return to Love: Reflections on the Principles of "A Course in Miracles"* (New York: Harper, 1996), 190–91.

4. Rick Reilly, commentary on ESPN.com, March 29, 2011. http://sports. espn.go.com/espn/news/story?id=6266899.

3. Unity

1. Dick Vitale, http://sports/espn.go.com/espn/dickvitale/news/story?id= 5059930, 4/6/2010.

2. See Jerome Schaum, http://www.blogsouthwest.com/blog/teamwork, 12/11/06.

3. See David Woods's article, http://www.butler.edu/absolutenm/templates/? a=1077&z=22, 3/19/09.

4. Servanthood

1. Robert Greenleaf, "The Servant as Leader" at http:/www.greenleaf.org/ whatissl/ (Westfield, IN: The Greenleaf Center for Servant Leadership, 2008). Originally published in 1970.

2. See David Woods, "Ronald Nored: Student Athlete, Student Teacher," *Indianapolis Star,* 12/2/2011.

5. Thankfulness

1. http://psychology.ucdavis.edu/Labs/emmons/PWT/index.cfm?Section=4 accessed 10/15/12.

2. Johnson Oatman Jr., "Count Your Blessings," in *Songs for Young People*, by Edwin Excell (Chicago, IL, 1897).

6. Accountability

1. John Miller, *QBQ! The Question Behind the Question: Practicing Personal Accountability at Work and in Life* (Putnam Publishing Group, 2004).

2. Brad Stevens, interview by David Letterman, *Late Show with David Letterman,* CBS, 8/7/10.

CPSIA information can be obtained at www.ICGtesting.com
Printed in the USA
LVOW10s0834310713

345430LV00002B/3/P